It Only
Hurts
on *Monday*

Why Pastors Quit and
What You Can Do About It

by
DR. GARY L. MCINTOSH
DR. ROBERT L. EDMONDSON

Carol Stream, IL 60188
1-800-253-4276

Published by ChurchSmart Resources

We are an Evangelical christian publisher committed to producing excellent products at affordable prices to help church leaders accomplish effective ministry in the areas of Church planting, Church growth, Church renewal and Leadership development.

For a free catalog of our resources call 1-800-253-4276.

Cover design by: Julie Becker
Manuscript edited by: Kimberly Miller

ISBN 1-889638-02-1

Dedication

Bob: To Pastor Mark Suko,

Who never quits.

Gary: To the loving members of Grace Baptist Church, San Bernardino, California. While serving as your pastor from 1976 to 1983, your supportive encouragement provided me with many happy Mondays.

Contents

It Only Hurts On Monday

PASTORS ARE QUITTING. Some are leaving for what they hope will be greener pastures in another church. Some are dropping out of ministry altogether. Why? Because they are hurting.

A fellow pastor always worked on Monday, the traditional "pastors' day off." We asked him why and will never forget his answer. "I always feel lousy on Monday, and if I am going to feel lousy, I may as well do it on church time!" That said it all.

The pressures of ministry are such that many pastors spend their day off simply trying to recover. We asked another pastor how he was getting along in his ministry. His wry answer was, "It only hurts on Monday."

On The Move

Evidence suggests that pastors are moving or dropping out at an increasing rate. Some experts estimate that just over two years is the average pastoral tenure.[1] Other estimates vary. The well respected Barna Research Group found that the average pastorate twenty years ago was about seven years in length but had dropped by 1993 to about four.[2]

Studies indicate a startling attrition rate among pastors in the Southern Baptist Convention, America's largest Protestant denomination.

> The latest statistics, garnered from the 1991 Uniform Church Letter, show the average pastoral tenure in the SBC is 5.5 years. A 4.3 average was reported in 1975. It rose to 4.6 years in 1980, and to 5.1 years in1985.
>
> But since the "average" figures include extremely long tenures ... denominational statistics specialist Jim Lowery of the Board's Corporate Planning and Research Department said a better gauge might be the "median" pastoral tenure–the middle value when half the cases are above and half are below. The number stood at 2.6 years in 1975, 2.7 years in 1980, 3.1 years in 1985 and 3.4 years in 1991 ...
>
> The most recent statistic on forced terminations–according to research conducted by the Sunday School Board in 1988– showed 116 pastors fired each month by Southern Baptist congregations... "I don't see any sign of these numbers decreasing," commented Norris Smith, a church staff support consultant at the Sunday School Board.[3]

Dr. Thom Rainer, dean of the Billy Graham School of Missions, Evangelism and Church Growth of the Southern Baptist Theological Seminary in Louisville, Kentucky, says that the average tenure for pastors among all Protestant churches is 2.3 years.[4]

The trend toward extremely short pastorates has telling effects on churches. Effective leadership takes time to develop. Too often it never gets a chance. Megachurch researcher Dr. John N. Vaughan suggests, "Pastors of small churches tend to change congregations more frequently than those that grow larger. Such mobility can reduce the ability to develop the confidence in ministry skills associated with longevity."[5] The Barna Research Group finds the short tenure of pastors alarming for two reasons. Not only do we seem to be losing many pastors, but research indicates that the most effective churches are those in which the pastor stays for a long time.[6] Kennon Callahan agrees with this observation, suggesting that any pastorate of less than seven years is "cost-ineffective."[7] A church's effectiveness in evangelism also appears to be linked to pastoral longevity. After studying 576 of the most evangelistic churches in North America, Thom Rainer explains,

> The church's evangelistic fervor often became a reality four to six years after the pastor began his ministry at that church. We found that older evangelistic churches tend to have pastors whose ministry is ten or more years ... We conclude, therefore, that leading a long-standing traditional church to evangelistic effectiveness requires leadership by example, tenacity, and longevity.[8]

Any church member who has lived through one or more short pastorates knows the problems created when a pastor leaves prematurely. Attendance drops off. So does giving. Questions and disputes arise. The church struggles for direction. Moreover, a church cannot simply pick up where it left off once the new pastor is hired. Building trust takes time. If there has been strife, healing takes even more time. Many attest to the sense that much of the ministry during this period is simply "on hold."

While there are certainly valid reasons for moving from one church to another, or for leaving vocational ministry altogether, there are also many unfortunate and avoidable ones. Many pastors complain about the consumer mentality with which parishioners approach church, the varied expectations of the different generations,[9] and the difficulty of ministry in an age of entertainment and superstars. Others point to the declining moral climate in our country, a climate which sadly produces its share of pastoral casualties. Still others say that the pastorate simply does not pay enough to survive.

Why do pastors leave churches? What causes many to leave the ministry completely? Perhaps more important, what can we do about it? These are the main questions we address in *It Only Hurts On Monday: Why Pastors Quit and What You Can Do About It.*

Exploring the Issues

Many of the causes of pastoral mobility and dropout can be found in the nature of today's church environment. *It Only Hurts On Monday* explores nine problems faced by modern pastors. These are burnout, professional isolation, inadequate education, unrealistic expectations, resistance to change, poor pastoral accountability, tight finances, personal loneliness, and spiritual warfare. We will also look at four pressures which constitute weekly "facts of life" for the average pastor. These include the pressure of never being quite "off duty," the pressure of too often being in "crisis mode," the pressure of being responsible for more than one controls, and the pressure of an inadequate measure of success. The latter is made more acute by the unique way in which pastors are measured as *Christians* by their performance on the job.

These issues are more than academic to us. As pastors we have both experienced, to some extent, all of the problems and pressures about which we write. We have known many painful Mondays and have struggled through a period of time during which we felt certain that we belonged in a different career. Moreover, we have known many pastors whose own doubts mirrored our own. Sadly, some of them are no longer in the ministry.

The combination of our experience, research, and hands-on contact with pastors and churches provides us a distinctive viewpoint from which to address this crucial issue of modern-day church life.

During 1995, Bob surveyed 30 ex-pastors from many church backgrounds to determine the reasons they left their church ministries. Thirty churches which had recently undergone a pastoral change responded to a second survey. While similar to the survey distributed to pastors, the second one sought to discover the church's point of view regarding pastoral change. Based on the information gained from the two surveys, Bob later conducted personal interviews to gain a clearer perspective on why pastors leave churches and what can be done about it. These surveys confirm that virtually all pastors struggle with one or more of the issues listed in this book.

God has placed Gary in the unique position of having frequent contact with pastors and churches going through pastoral change. In his personal church consulting practice, and as director of the Talbot

Doctor of Ministry program (Biola University), Gary has counseled pastors and churches on a variety of issues for the last thirteen years. He has discovered that the question of when to leave a church is a major one for pastors. He first addressed this question in a 1986 article in *Leadership*, "Deciding To Leave."[10] Along with Bob's research, Gary brings years of practical experience among more than 50 denominations and church associations.

The stories contained in *It Only Hurts On Monday* are true. In order to protect the identities of the churches and pastors involved, names and certain other details have been altered. In some cases stories have been combined and composite characters used. However, the accounts represent actual events.

Addressing the problems that tempt pastors to quit is supremely important for the sake of pastors as well as the churches they serve. It is not enough to merely identify the problems. Churches and pastors need solutions. For this reason, each chapter includes a section entitled "You Can Help!" Whether you are a pastor or church member, acting on even a few of these suggestions will make your church ministry a good deal more encouraging. Your efforts may even encourage a pastor to stay and to serve longer, which will benefit both your church and the pastor's life greatly.

Many parishioners view pastors as unique people in a unique job. Pastors have a calling, not a career. While this is certainly true, you may be surprised to learn that some of the issues with which pastors struggle are common to other professions as well. We begin with one such issue: burnout.

–End Introduction–

[1]Louis McBurney, Every Pastor Needs a Pastor (Waco, TX: Word Books, 1977), 73.

[2]George Barna, Today's Pastors: A Revealing Look at What Pastors Are Saying about Themselves, Their Peers and the Pressures They Face (Ventura, CA: Regal Books, Gospel Light, 1993), 36.

[3]Chip Alford, "Pastor, Church Must Overcome Barriers for Long Tenure," *Facts & Trends*, March 1992, 8.

[4]Dr. Thom Rainer, Effective Evangelistic Churches (Nashville: Broadman & Holman, 1996), 43-44.

[5]John N. Vaughan, Megachurches & America's Cities (Grand Rapids: Baker Books, 1993), 90.

[6]Barna, Today's Pastors, 36.

[7]Kennon L. Callahan, Twelve Keys to an Effective Church: Strategic Planning for Mission (San Francisco: Harper & Row, 1983), 51.

[8]Rainer, 43-44.

[9]Gary L. McIntosh, Three Generations: Riding The Waves of Change In Your Church (Grand Rapids: Revell, 1995).

[10]Gary L. McIntosh, "Deciding To Leave," Leadership Journal, Summer, 1986.

Chapter One

When The Lights Won't Turn On

THE ELECTRIC LIGHT is a source of great convenience, allowing us to function at night as if it were the middle of the day. Unfortunately, the electric light also causes us minor irritation when it burns out. It is frustrating to enter a darkened room and flip the familiar wall switch expecting the room to be filled with warm light only to be disappointed.

What happens when the light won't turn on? Not much really. The power is still on. The switch works. The wiring is fine. Even the light bulb itself is 95% intact. Only a tiny wire strand called a filament has broken. Yet because of this minor change, none of the system designed to bring light to a darkened room will function.

Many pastors are in approximately the same condition. They still have the power that at other times has made them a light to those they serve (Matt. 5:16), yet some subtle change has taken place within them. Although they are outwardly intact, they no longer seem to radiate that same energy. The power is available to them, but it is not flowing as it once did. They are tired, unhappy, and often ready to quit. They are "burned out." Burnout is one reason why pastors leave churches. Consider Pastor Tony and Wanda, his wife.

One Pastor's Story

Tony turned his Mazda onto the interstate ramp. He and his family rode in silence. No one was in the mood to talk. This was no vacation, no weekend visit to relatives. They were leaving for good. Tony had resigned from the Valley Community Church after prolonged conflict with the established (and entrenched) leadership there.

It was a rough four years punctuated by difficult business meetings and cold comments. Tony wanted nothing more than to lead the church into greater effectiveness in ministry. The changes he initiated were modest and his leadership style was anything but dictatorial. Nevertheless, he met with resistance at every turn. The ghosts of former pastors loomed large in the rooms of the old church building. Tony and Wanda regularly felt that they were measured against a rose-colored image of a previous pastoral family and found wanting. In this environment, they sought to minister to an aging congregation whose love was reserved for a bygone era. They comforted the grieving, listened to the complaining, and mediated between the bickering. Yet there were few rewards and even less appreciation.

As if life was not difficult enough for this struggling couple, Wanda's health began to deteriorate. Doctors diagnosed her problem as a degenerative condition requiring surgery. Her recovery was slow. Paying off the bills on Tony's salary was even slower.

Wanda's convalescence was made more difficult because the move to this rural parish had taken Tony and Wanda away from their families. They felt the pain of loneliness, a pain only partially deadened by the fellowship of friends and colleagues.

For Tony and Wanda, the joy of ministry faded. The light went out. Things came to a head between Tony and one of the board members. This man was not about to submit to Tony's leadership and, moreover, busied himself at every turn trying to thwart his pastor's plans. Tony could not muster the support to effectively counter his efforts, let alone discipline him for his divisive behavior. Without the backing of the rest of the board, he felt he had little recourse but to resign. Now here he was, driving down the interstate with his family toward an uncertain future. He had no intention of reentering ministry. He was through, beaten. His biggest question now was, "How will I feed my family?" Other than death, he and Wanda agreed that nothing worse could happen to them.

Today Tony and Wanda both recognize that they had a distorted point of view. They were simply unable to see beyond their problems with an eternal perspective. They had no sense of assurance that God was at work in any of their painful experiences. This distorted and subjective thinking is the very essence of burnout.

A Seven-Letter Word

"Burnout" is a popular term with good reason—it's descriptive. It fits the way most people feel from time to time. Because of this, burnout has become an umbrella word commonly used to describe maladies ranging from simple frustration or boredom to clinical depression.

As an excuse, burnout has few rivals. After all, who can argue when someone backs out of a commitment claiming that he is feeling burned out? How can anyone else assess the accuracy of such a claim? Who wants to risk causing the serious consequences that a burned-out individual could suffer? Consequently, "Burnout" is the trump card for excuse-makers everywhere. It legitimizes our lack of endurance and commitment in an age in which "our attention spans have been conditioned by thirty-second commercials [and] our sense of reality has been flattened by thirty-page abridgments."[1]

The term burnout has become polluted by misuse and overuse until it is almost meaningless. That is unfortunate since there are those to whom the term quite correctly applies. Many people say they are burned out. Some actually are. A definition is in order. The dictionary defines "burnout" as "exhaustion of physical or emotional strength or motivation usually as a result of prolonged stress or frustration."[2] Stanley J. Modic cites research which indicates that true "burnout" consists of physical, emotional, and mental exhaustion seen in identifiable symptoms.

> Physical exhaustion is characterized by low energy, chronic fatigue, and a feeling of weakness. People approaching burnout are more accident-prone, are increasingly susceptible to illnesses, nagging colds, nausea, muscle tension and back pains, and undergo changes in eating habits.

> Emotional exhaustion primarily involves feelings of helplessness, hopelessness, and being trapped. In extreme cases these feelings can lead to emotional breakdown, or thoughts about suicide.

> Mental exhaustion includes the development of negative attitudes toward one's self, work, or life. Burnout victims often feel inadequate, inferior, and incompetent, and exhibit a "who-gives-a-damn" attitude.[3]

Although these explanations are helpful, one element is lacking in our definition. As people created in the image of God, we are more than just physical, emotional, and mental beings. Part of our nature is also spiritual. As believers in Jesus Christ, we have the unlimited spiritual resources of God at our disposal! For a believer then, burnout also must involve an inability to make use of those resources.

How did the Apostle Paul avoid burnout? In more desperate straits than most of us are likely to encounter, he wrote, "We are hard pressed on every side, but not crushed; perplexed, but not in despair;

persecuted, but not abandoned; struck down, but not destroyed" (2 Cor. 4:8-9).[4]

Hard pressed? No kidding! Paul wrote this letter during a period of his ministry that was at once the most fruitful and the most painful of any recorded in the New Testament. It included visits to now familiar places like Philippi, Thessalonica, Athens, Corinth, and Ephesus. Everywhere, Paul's preaching attracted converts and controversy. At Ephesus Paul's ministry actually caused a riot. Paul and his companions lived with the threat of death and were constantly "hard pressed ... perplexed ... persecuted ... struck down." In spite of all of this, he was able to write that he and his friends were "not crushed ... not in despair ... not abandoned ... not destroyed." Today, Paul might say, "We are down but not out." If anyone had a right to say, "I feel burned out," it would be Paul. Yet he and his friends found in their God a sufficient source of strength to go on.

It seems apparent that burnout for modern pastors involves an inability to make full use of this same source of strength. How else can one explain the casualty rates among pastors who undoubtedly face difficulty, but are novices at suffering compared to the apostles? Perhaps many of today's pastors have something in common with the psalmist who wrote, "I am like a man without strength. I am set apart with the dead, like the slain who lie in the grave, whom you remember no more, who are cut off from your care" (Ps. 88:4b-5). Perhaps, like the psalmist, modern burnout victims *lose faith* that God is even interested in their problems. Loss of faith is central to a biblical understanding of this malady. Burnout, then, is the exhaustion of physical, emotional, mental, *and spiritual* strength or motivation usually caused by prolonged stress or frustration *and inability to appropriate the full spiritual resources of God.*

When facing burnout, a pastor is facing a crisis of major proportions. Jesus asserted that the greatest commandment in the entire law was to "love the Lord your God with all your heart and with all your soul and with all your mind and with all your strength" (Mark 12:30). These four facets of our being—our heart, soul, mind, and strength—are the very facets exhausted when we are experiencing burnout. Therefore, when a pastor experiences burnout, he finds it difficult even to love God.

One common misconception about burnout is that it happens mostly to lazy people. This is simply not the case. While anyone can claim burnout as an excuse for laziness or a rationale for failure, true burnout occurs in the lives of those who make no excuses. Burnout is the disease of the motivated and the conscientious. Dr. Herbert J. Freudenberger, author of *Burn-Out: The High Cost of High Achievement*, writes,

> [Burnout is] a problem born of good intentions. The people who fall prey to it are, for the most part, decent individuals who have striven hard to reach a goal. Their schedules are busy, and whatever the project or job, they can be counted on to do more than their share. They're usually the leaders among us who have never been able to admit to limitations.[5]

Good intentions ... busy schedules ... leaders among us. Does this sound like anyone you know? Pastors are prime candidates for this modern malaise. Statistics from a survey of pastors conducted at Fuller Seminary reveal that 75% reported having at least one significant crisis due to stress. Eighty percent believed that ministry is affecting their families negatively. Ninety percent felt inadequately trained to meet the demands of the job, and 50% felt unable to do so.[6] Another survey of over four thousand Protestant ministers found that 58% felt that the work of the church seemed futile.[7] It comes as no surprise that in our survey of pastors who have recently moved out of ministry, we found that 40% were experiencing burnout.[8]

Why Now?

The pastorate has always been challenging work, so why are we talking about burnout now? Is there something in today's church environment that causes more pain to those who lead the flock than at other times in church history? Haven't pastors always been subject to spiritual struggle and attack by the evil one? It is true that spiritual and emotional struggles are part of the definition of pastoral work. Paul summed it all up at the end of his ministry: "I have fought the good fight, I have finished the race, I have kept the faith" (2 Tim. 4:7). He clearly did not consider his experience unique. On the contrary, he passed the baton to his protégé Timothy when he urged him to "fight the good fight of the faith" (1 Tim. 1:18). His letters to Timothy elaborate on that concept. "Preach the Word; be prepared in season and out of season; correct, rebuke, and encourage—with great patience and careful instruction" (2 Tim. 4:2). "Watch your life and doctrine closely. Persevere in them, because if you do, you will save both yourself and your hearers" (1 Tim. 4:16). These passages as well as others tell

15

us that the New Testament concept of pastoral work involves intense spiritual and emotional struggle. Each generation of pastors learns this firsthand.

Stress and frustration, then, are not the key factors determining who will burn out and who will not. Rather, it is a pastor's *response* to stress and frustration that makes the difference. Pastors have always needed a pattern of personal spiritual disciplines in order to keep their perspective when times were difficult. Oswald Sanders, a well known Bible conference speaker and prolific writer, observes, "It stands clear in the book of Acts that the leaders who significantly influenced the Christian movement were men who were filled with the Holy Spirit."[9] Such men gave themselves to "prayer and the ministry of the word" (Acts 6:4).

Herein lies the problem. It is extremely difficult for a pastor of a modern church to give himself in any consistent way to these biblical priorities. Modern pastors face ever-increasing demands. With committees, counseling, calling, Bible studies, bulletins, and building programs, the pastor's job as commonly conceived today is wide ranging indeed. In this demanding environment, the press of church affairs often squeezes communion with God out of a pastor's schedule. The apostles considered the strength drawn from communion with God to be essential. Even headstrong and independent Peter wrote, "If anyone speaks, he should do it as one speaking the very words of God. If anyone serves, he should do it in the strength God provides ..." (1 Pet. 4:11). Many modern pastors seem to lack this strength. Their lives are so hectic, they lose sight of the priorities voiced by the earliest church leaders. Consider how this pattern frequently develops.

High hopes accompany the start of any new job and the pastorate is no exception. When a pastor begins in a new place of ministry, the optimism, if it were seawater, could float a battleship. Often the church has not only a great sense of joy (and relief) at the calling of a new pastor,[10] but also a set of exaggerated expectations.[11] Kent Hughes describes the joy of this honeymoon phase of ministry as he personally experienced it.

> Optimism ran high. As the fair-haired boy, I was told by friends that great things were about to happen, and it would not be long before the new church would be larger than its mother. Such talk enlarged my expectations. I believed it...

> From the start, we had everything going for us. We had the prayers and predictions of our friends who believed a vast, growing work was inevitable. We had the sophisticated insights of the science of church growth. We had a superb nucleus of believers. And we had *me*, a young pastor with a good track record who was entering his prime. We expected to grow.[12]

These feelings of promise and hope are familiar to any pastor beginning a new place of ministry. Unfortunately they are often only temporary. The honeymoon does not last. There is a natural process whereby the pastor moves from the role of a learner to that of a leader. That's when things can get difficult.

> It is significant to note that when a new pastor arrives in a church he is realistically dependent on the knowledge and leadership of the people. When he is able to establish himself and has become acquainted with the congregation, his own need to control becomes more important. The honeymoon ends as his dependency tapers off and he begins taking over the reins.[13]

The ensuing difficulties vary in nature. Not only are there leadership issues to face when the honeymoon is over, but there are more "people issues." Now that folks feel they can trust the new pastor, they will more easily come and share their burdens with him. With domestic problems increasingly prevalent among Christians, a modern pastor is literally "Called into Crisis."[14]

The result of this new and more demanding atmosphere is a set of impossibilities. The pastor is expected to bring about great things for the church, but he has little authority to do so. He is frequently expected to involve himself in an ever-increasing array of activities designed to meet the "needs" of his people. However, he still has only twenty-four hours per day.

Because of his efforts to meet extrabiblical demands, he may fail to meet the biblical ones. Church members rightly expect him to be a tower of spiritual and emotional strength, but his reserves are often low because of what one pastor bluntly called a "distorted concept of the ministry."[15] This is the environment that burns pastors out.

It is not a small problem. Evidence is mounting that the demands of the modern pastorate are destroying its practitioners. A survey conducted by *Leadership* indicated that 63% of pastors viewed congregational expectations as detrimental to their marriage. Eighty-one percent said that ministry left them with insufficient time with their spouse.[16] "Some studies of clergy suggest as many as 75% of the clergy experience regular periods of major distress, while 33% have seriously considered leaving the ministry."[17] Barna concludes, "We appear to be losing many pastors after relatively brief careers in full-time ministry."[18]

The ironic truth that many pastors are too busy doing church work to maintain their own spiritual equilibrium is not often understood by church members. They correctly look to their pastor for spiritual leadership and therefore assume that he is spiritually healthy. As one layman put it, "We pay you not to have problems."[19] The assumption that he is spiritually "on top" may be erroneous. Despite his confident public demeanor, he may be empty inside and nearing a cave-in. No one can unswervingly minister for God without taking time to be with God.

The Results of Burnout

It is important that pastoral burnout be prevented. There is more at stake than the well-being of one man. The pastor is not the only one in trouble when burnout occurs. His burnout harms the church he serves in numerous ways. Here are three:

An Unmotivated Leader

A burned-out pastor is by definition an unmotivated leader. "Motive implies an emotion or desire operating on the will and causing it to act."[20] Internal motivation is necessary to the pastorate. "The young man of leadership caliber will work while others waste time, study while others sleep, pray while others play."[21] A burned-out person is one who has lost this motivation.

> It's 6 a.m. You lie in bed cringing from the thought of crawling out of bed. The idea of calling in sick flashes across your mind. You dismiss it; there are too many appointments and meetings lined up.
>
> The splashing water of the shower does little to invigorate you. Day after day, the mirror reflects a slump in the shoulders, a furrowed brow, bags under the eyes. Leaving to brave another day, you know what's ahead—too many details, too many interruptions, too much work ... too few rewards.[22]

Alistair Brown, pastor of the Gerrard Street Baptist Church in Aberdeen, Scotland, suggests that pastors in a state of exhaustion often wonder if the effort is really worth it. He notes that at such times one of the easiest mental distractions is to begin composing a resignation letter.[23] The perception of futility brought on by burnout creates a desire to escape. Forty percent of the pastors responding to our survey cited burnout as a cause of their recent resignation.

What kind of leadership can a pastor offer a church when inwardly he suspects that his work is futile? How can he enthusiastically lead when he must fight an increasing desire to escape his responsibilities? A leader must maintain his own motivation and inspire and motivate others. Sanders comments on this aspect of leadership.

> The power of inspiring others to service and sacrifice will mark God's leader. His incandescence sets those around him alight. Charles Cowman not only achieved a prodigious amount of work himself but possessed the ability to inject the spirit of work into those with whom he was associated. His zeal and drive were infectious.[24]

Paul urged Timothy to "set an example for the believers in speech, in life, in love, in faith, and in purity ... Watch your life and doctrine closely. Persevere in them, because if you do, you will save both yourself and your hearers" (1 Tim. 4:12,16). Unfortunately, when burnout comes, the ability to inspire others by example goes.

A pastoral acquaintance has an unusually strong ability to inspire others. He gathers leaders around him and things just happen. As a result of his strong pastoral gifts, he has successfully established a new church and has seen it grow to over seven hundred in attendance. A few years ago he went through a period of burnout. One consequence of his exhaustion was that his ability to lead by influencing and inspiring others faltered. Church leaders no longer seemed enthused by his ideas. For the first time in a fifteen-year ministry, major initiatives failed to pass muster with the congregation. The growth of the church slowed. All of this resulted from the change within him like that in a burned-out light bulb. The spiritual zeal that had given life to his leadership was temporarily lacking. As a result, the whole church suffered.

An Unproductive Leader

A burned-out pastor is also an unproductive leader. God has appointed leaders in a church for a reason. The fortunes of a given ministry rise and fall with the presence or absence of visionary leadership.[25] "Burned-out" and "visionary leadership" are mutually exclusive terms. A church cannot expect the kind of forward-looking leadership so necessary to a healthy church from a burned-out, ready-to-quit pastor. Quite the opposite.

> In burnout, the victim becomes demoralized and knows things are not going right. People are not affirming him. He begins to lose the vision. He suffers from loss of hope. Burnout often results in a disengagement from the main task. It often has symptoms of depersonalization and detachment. And a state of crushing discouragement–almost despair–sets in. Demoralization is a good way to summarize it.[26]

One pastor in advanced stages of burnout fell into the habit of spending hours staring out of his office window in an effort to catch supermarket shoppers parking in the church lot.[27] Burnout reduced him to a highly paid parking lot attendant. Once again, the effect on the church is obvious. A church with an unproductive leader will not easily claim new ground for the kingdom of God.

A Frequent Mover

Finally, a burned-out pastor is a frequent mover. Tony and Wanda are an example. Valley Church was not the first church from which Tony had resigned in a state of burnout. His previous church had also given his family more than their share of hard knocks. He had become the latest in a long line of pastors to stay in that church for three years or less. Tony experienced two pastorates of less than four years each. He burned out in both places and finally left ministry altogether.

Evidence suggests that burnout is a contributing factor in the resignations of as many as 40% of pastors.[28] Most of these men move on to other churches in search of a situation in which they can be effective. This is not only unhealthy for the church, it is also unhealthy for the pastor. Among other things, it severely limits his professional development. If a pattern of burnout causes a pattern of moving, it allows a pastor to stop growing in his profession. He simply repeats his ministry again in another place.

> It has been said that it is far more honest for a pastor who has been in the ministry for fifteen years to say that he has had three years' experience five times over rather than to say that he has had fifteen years' experience.

Short pastorates have not only kept ministers from developing skills which come from length of time in one location, but have also made it possible for ministers to continue to make the same mistakes over and over again. Bad habits developed in the first pastorate are often repeated in the second, third, and fourth.[29]

The writer to the Hebrews urged his readers to make their leaders' work a joy and not a burden, adding that a joyless leader is of "no advantage" to the church (Heb. 13:17). Making a pastor's work less frustrating might encourage him to stay and grow as a leader. Early in my ministry I experienced a period of exhaustion bordering on burnout. One Sunday during worship a particular song touched me and I wept openly. It was unlike me. One of the leaders noticed and approached me to voice his concern that I was working too hard and needed to delegate more. His genuine statement of care lifted my spirits considerably.

A shepherd can never become a competent leader to his sheep if his constant frustration has him regularly in search of another flock. A little encouragement can motivate him to stay with the flock he has. He then can grow and develop in ways that would otherwise be impossible. The advantages to the church are clear.

When the pastor suffers from burnout, the whole church suffers. The mere fact of short tenures is more harmful to churches than most people know. It takes time to build relationships. It takes time to build momentum. It takes time to develop the chemistry that can make a church something more than a group of people who meet on Sunday. A wise church will take steps to help remedy the situation, not just for the pastor's sake, but for the sake of the entire church.

Tony and Wanda are still out of full-time ministry. Tony works as an administrator; Wanda is a receptionist. Both speak occasionally of a desire to get back into the ministry, and yet there is something vaguely unsettling to them about the prospect of another pastorate. Neither is sanguine about placing themselves or their children at risk of being hurt again. How many Tonys are out there? How many Wandas wait for them to come home? How many pastoral couples find their strength slowly ebbing away as a result of the realities of modern church life? How many pastors will resign, perhaps never to pastor again? What about your pastor? Is the light still shining brightly?

You Can Help!

If more people recognized the symptoms of burnout, it wouldn't be the problem that it is. Unfortunately, the victims of burnout usually didn't see it coming. Ironically, those around them usually did. Dr. Herbert J. Freudenberger offers a simple test to help a person determine if he or she is a candidate for burnout. His test requires looking back on the past six months or so and evaluating life at the office, in social situations, and at home.

Allow about 30 seconds for each answer. Then assign it a number from 1 (for no or little change) to 5 (for a great deal of change) to designate the degree of change you perceive.

1. Do you tire more easily?
    Feel fatigued rather than energetic?   1 2 3 4 5

2. Are people annoying you by telling you,
    "You don't look too good lately"?   1 2 3 4 5

3. Are you working harder and harder and
    accomplishing less and less?   1 2 3 4 5

4. Are you increasingly cynical and disenchanted?   1 2 3 4 5

5. Are you often invaded by a sadness
    you can't explain?   1 2 3 4 5

6. Are you forgetting? (appointments,
    deadlines, personal possessions)   1 2 3 4 5

7. Are you increasingly irritable?
    More short-tempered?
    More disappointed in the people around you?   1 2 3 4 5

8. Are you seeing close friends and family
    members less frequently?   1 2 3 4 5

9. Are you too busy to do even routine things
    like make phone calls or read reports or send
    out your Christmas cards?   1 2 3 4 5

10. Are you suffering from physical complaints?
    (aches, pains, headaches, a lingering cold)   1 2 3 4 5

11. Do you feel disoriented when the activity
of the day comes to a halt?　　　　　1　2　3　4　5

12. Is joy elusive?　　　　　1　2　3　4　5

13. Are you unable to laugh at a joke about yourself? 1　2　3　4　5

14. Does sex seem like more trouble than it's worth? 1　2　3　4　5

15. Do you have very little to say to people?　　1　2　3　4　5

. . .

0-25　　　You're doing fine.

26-35　　There are things you should be watching.

36-50　　You're a candidate.

51-65　　You are burning out.

Over 65　You're in a dangerous place, threatening to your physical
and mental well-being.[30]

. . . . .

Those close to the victim of burnout can often see many of these symptoms before he can. How is your pastor doing? If you have some concerns, here are some ways you can help.

1. **Hold him accountable for stress management disciplines like rest, exercise, and meaningful recreation.**

Monday, the typical pastor's day of rest, is not the best day off for some pastors. Sunday's efforts require the expenditure of large amounts of emotional energy. Adrenaline flows and the next day is a natural valley after that mountaintop experience.[31] Some pastors need to work through that low point of the week by taking care of low-stress tasks in the office. That way they don't inflict their poor mood on their families on their only day at home. Paradoxically, such a person may rest better when his mind and spirit are more at ease than they are on the day after Sunday. Whether it be Monday or another day, see to it that your pastor takes his days off, along with his vacations. Make sure he actually gets away and does something unrelated to ministry.

2. Protect him from spiritual leeches. Every church has its "clinging vines."[32]

These are people who seem to drain the energy right out of those around them. They seek someone stronger to provide them with the sense of well-being they cannot maintain on their own. The pastor is their natural target. He can handle some of this load, but not all of it and not forever. Surround him with some kind of protection. This may take the form of a secretary who makes appointments and screens calls or a group of leaders who can help bear the load of counseling. Church members can protect the pastor by taking those troublesome and needy souls into their hearts and discipling them, thus lessening their dependence on the pastor.

3. Get him to go with his strengths.

Everyone has inborn strengths and God-given talents. The problem with the pastorate is that it is often such a generalized role that a man can spend an inordinate amount of time working outside the sphere of his gifts. This is always frustrating. Find out what your pastor does naturally well, what he likes to do, and encourage him in that area. Take some of the other tasks away from him by volunteering to do them yourself or finding someone else who will. If you are a board member, suggest rewriting the job description to fit the man you hired. Sometimes simply praising him in the area of his strengths will encourage him to spend more time in those areas and thus lessen his stress.

4. Get him together with other pastors.

Require it of him. Isolation contributes to burnout. Gathering with other pastors helps to eliminate the sense of being out there all alone. See to it that pastors' conferences and seminars are part of the church budget. He will thank you for it.

–End Chapter One–

[1]Eugene H. Peterson, A Long Obedience in the Same Direction: Discipleship in an Instant Society (Downers Grove, IL: InterVarsity Press, 1980), 11-12.

[2]Merriam Webster's Collegiate Dictionary, 10th ed., s.v. "burnout."

[3]Ayala Pines and Elliot Aronson, Career Burnout: Causes and Cures (New York: The Free Press); quoted in Stanley J. Modic, "Surviving Burnout: The Malady of Our Age," Industry Week, 20 February 1989: 30-31.

[4]Unless otherwise noted, all Scripture quotations are from The Holy Bible: New International Version, Copyright 1973, 1978, 1984 by International Bible Society.

[5]Herbert J. Freudenberger with Geraldine Richelson, Burn-Out: The High Cost of High Achievement (Garden City, NY: Anchor Press, 1980), 11-12.

[6]Richard A. Blackmon, "Survey of Pastors," in "The Hazards of the Ministry," Psy.D. diss., Graduate School of Psychology, Fuller Theological Seminary, Pasadena, CA, 1984.

[7]John E. Biersdorf, "A New Model of Ministry," in Creating an Intentional Ministry, ed. John E. Biersdorf (Nashville, TN: Abingdon Press, 1976), 23; quoted in Edward B. Bratcher, The Walk-on-Water Syndrome: Dealing with Professional Hazards in the Ministry, with a foreword by Wayne Oates (Waco, TX: Word Books, Word, Inc., 1984), 9.

[8]Pastoral Survey, see appendix.

[9]J. Oswald Sanders, Spiritual Leadership (Chicago: Moody Press, 1967), 72.

[10]Henry A. Virkler, Choosing a New Pastor: The Complete Handbook (Nashville, TN: Oliver Nelson, Thomas Nelson, 1992), 170.

[11]H.B. London, Jr. & Neil B. Wiseman, Pastors at Risk: Help for Pastors, Hope for the Church (Wheaton, IL: Victor Books, Scripture Press Publications, 1993), 40.

[12]Kent and Barbara Hughes, Liberating Ministry from the Success Syndrome (Wheaton, IL: Tyndale House Publishers, 1988), 18.

[13]Louis McBurney, Every Pastor Needs a Pastor (Waco, TX: Word Books, 1977), 73.

[14]James D. Berkley, Called into Crisis: The Nine Greatest Challenges of Pastoral Care (Carol Stream, IL and Dallas: Christianity Today and Word Publishing, 1989), 10.

[15]Charles U. Wagner, The Pastor: His Life and Work (Schaumburg, IL: Regular Baptist Press, 1976), 11.

[16]David Goetz, "Is the Pastor's Family Safe at Home?" Leadership: A Practical Journal for Church Leaders 13, no. 4 (Fall 1992): 39-41.

[17]Malony and Hunt, "The Psychology of Clergy" quoted in London and Wiseman, Pastors at Risk, 163.

[18]Barna, Today's Pastors, 40.

[19]Laile E. Bartlett, The Vanishing Parson (Boston: Beacon Press, 1971), 127; quoted in Bratcher, The Walk-On-Water Syndrome, 85.

[20]Merriam Webster's Collegiate Dictionary, s.v. "motive."

[21]Sanders, Spiritual Leadership, 45.

[22]Modic, "Surviving Burnout," 29.

[23]Alistair Brown, "When You Feel Empty," Leadership Journal 11, no. 3 (Summer 1990): 119.

[24]Sanders, Spiritual Leadership, 68; referring to L. B. Cowman, Charles E. Cowman, 269.

[25]George Barna, The Power of Vision: How You Can Capture and Apply God's Vision for Your Ministry (Ventura, CA: Regal Books, Gospel Light, 1992), 11.

[26]Archibald Hart, Professor of Psychology and Dean of the Graduate School of Psychology at Fuller Seminary; interview by London and Wiseman, in Pastors at Risk, 162.

[27]Hart; interview by London and Wiseman, in Pastors at Risk, 165.

[28]Pastoral Survey, see appendix.

[29]Bratcher, The Walk-On-Water Syndrome, 164.

[30]Freudenberger with Richelson, Burn-Out, 17-18.

[31]London and Wiseman, Pastors at Risk, 168-169.

[32]London and Wiseman, Pastors at Risk, 170.

Chapter Two

When Are You Going To Get A Real Job?

"MY KIDS DON'T KNOW how to explain to their friends what it is I do. One of 'em is always asking me, 'Hey Dad, when are you going to get a real job?'"

Del Wilson laughed at the speaker's joke along with everyone else. A prominent professor at a prominent seminary, the seminar speaker had years of pastoral experience and with it, first-hand knowledge of what every pastor knows very well: that the pastorate is unlike any other career.

Even as he laughed, Del remembered that he had entered the ministry precisely because he had expected it to be different than other jobs. Del's high school commitment to Christ had taken on new meaning in college as a group of joyous Christians had taken him "under their wing" and discipled him. He decided to enroll in Bible college, be trained in the Word, and find God's will for his life. Del found heroes there: pastors and missionaries. He began to believe that, next to the ministry, all other occupations were second-rate.

The words of a chapel speaker rang in his ears: "If God calls you to be a preacher, don't stoop to be a king!" In his youthful simplicity, he interpreted statements like these to mean that the ministry was superior to any other job, period. He never considered the all important caveat: *If God calls you.* He knew only that he wanted his life to count for God and it appeared that the ministry was the best and possibly the only way to make it count. In fact, the more he thought about it, the more it seemed that any other career would just be a way to make money so that he could serve Christ in his spare time. Thus, with little consideration for his gifts, he concluded that he was indeed called to the pastorate. Later when he realized that he had based this life-changing decision on false notions about the nature and significance of work, he began to doubt his call to ministry. His doubts worsened as he struggled to perform adequately in areas of ministry that lay outside the sphere of his gifts.

Del's idealistic notions of the pastorate had proven unrealistic. Today, it seemed that what set ministry apart from other careers was not spiritual superiority but impossible expectations! He laughed at the speaker's one-liner, but inwardly he asked himself that same question, "Del, when are you going to get a real job?"

What is the pastorate? Is it a career or a calling? Is it a living or a life? Is it a job or an adventure? In some ways it is like other professions. It has required tasks which result in a paycheck. It has frustrations and rewards. Pastors face the regular challenges of conflict management, time pressure, and limited resources. Pastors also know the reward of genuine appreciation from some if not all of their "customers." There is nothing unique about that. Still, in many important ways the pastorate is unique among careers. Further, its distinctive characteristics contribute to a high ministerial casualty rate.

The Odd Job

Some say that men tend to gain a sense of identity and worth from their job. If so, how does a pastor assess his identity and worth in a job that is different than those held by the people of his congregation? How does he work with people who have no firsthand experience with his job, yet who regularly assess his effectiveness in it? How does he measure his success as a professional when he tends to be isolated from others in his field? In these and other ways the pastorate is a unique career choice. Professional isolation is one factor that sometimes causes pastors to leave the ministry in favor of "a real job."

If church members could understand some of these dynamics, it would help them better appreciate their pastor. It might also alleviate some of his isolation—a stress that occasionally tempts pastors to sell insurance instead. Here are five ways in which the pastorate is the ultimate odd job.

Unique Calling

A pastor approaches his calling to the ministry differently than he would a decision to enter any other career. There are two ways in which the "calling to ministry" is unusual.

First, the calling is uniquely subjective. The New Testament says little about the calling of God to the gospel ministry. It seems to indicate that there is such a call and that it comes through or at least is accompanied by the recognition of the church and/or its leaders (Acts 13:2 and Titus 1:5). Scripture stresses the need for spiritual maturity (1 Tim. 3:1-7), and the right gifts (Rom. 12:8). A person's own desire to serve in this capacity is equally important (I Tim. 3:1; 1 Pet. 5:2).

These elements provide a healthy balance between the objective and subjective. A person's desire to enter ministry can be confirmed or denied by the presence or absence of observable qualities. By the same token, encouragement from others to consider ministry can be weighed against a person's own spirit-led desire. However, in today's ecclesiastical climate, this balance is often missing. We often neglect to consider carefully a person's talents.[1] The mysterious and subjective sense of calling outweighs all other considerations. Joe is a case in point.

> Joe was in his early forties and had been a practicing dentist for fifteen years. When he became dissatisfied with his role as a layman, Joe's pastor interpreted his dissatisfaction as an indication that God was calling him into "full-time Christian service." Without serious consideration of Joe's gifts, his pastor advised him to go to the seminary... It soon became obvious that he could not handle the academic pressures. Moreover, in his homiletics class he found that he could not organize his thoughts into a sermon, nor could he get up before an audience without becoming panic-stricken. Before long, Joe was in a serious state of depression. Thankfully, the supportive dean of students recognized Joe's trouble and helped him realize that what he had interpreted as God's call to a church-related vocation was based largely on the false assumption that to be a first-class Christian he needed to be a pastor.[2]

In no other field is a subjective experience viewed as more important than an objective evaluation of one's abilities. Joe would never have considered dentistry if shaky hands would have prevented him from developing skill with the drill. Yet he considered ministry without ever asking, "Do I have the ability to create and preach a sermon?" Only later did reality bring him up short. No one told him that a call must include desire *and* ability. Joe is not alone. Our survey of pastors who have recently resigned indicated that 27% have doubts about their callings.[3]

Unique Expectations

The pastorate is a "high and holy calling." Some parishioners treat it almost as if it were a superhuman role entrusted to people who are spiritually somewhere between humanity and deity. Edward Bratcher traces this perception of ministry to the Roman Catholic distinction between clergy and laity which asserted that laymen held "second-class status."[4] He further asserts that while Protestants have long since renounced this doctrine, replacing it with the priesthood of all believers, the pastoral office is still elevated in perception and practice.[5]

Many, if not most, of today's pastors have been taught a view of pastoral ministry which falsely puts the pastor on a pedestal from which he sooner or later must fall. This thinking is prevalent in much of this century's pastoral literature, for example:

> No seraph from glory was ever entrusted with so important an errand to the children of men as that for which the Son of God calls and commissions the ministers of His gospel. The exalted objects of the Christian Ministry give to the office a most exalted character. "Its grand aims," says Mr. Murphy, "are to exalt Jehovah, the Creator, Redeemer, and Judge of the world; to overthrow the power of Satan, the prince of all evil; to save mankind from sin and hell; to banish vice and all other evil from the earth; to bring true happiness to the lost children of Adam; to build up a glorious church amidst the ruins which sin has wrought; to prepare citizens for the heavenly world who shall behold all and share the infinite blessedness of the Son of God. Surely it must be a calling of no ordinary importance which God has appointed for such ends. Who can describe its solemn grandeur?"[6]

Is he talking about a job held by a mortal? If one attaches half the importance and responsibility to the pastorate as this passage seems to indicate, then the pastor is nothing less than an apprentice messiah! Such views create a good deal of tension when they collide with reality. Underneath that pastoral persona lives a mere human being.

Unfortunately it is not just the seminary that holds a superhuman view of the pastorate. Many in the congregation hold similarly unrealistic beliefs. The practical expectations of pastors and their families are often beyond reason. Ruth Truman in *Underground Manual for Ministers' Wives (And Other Bewildered Women)* sums up the role in part.

Some people believe there are three kinds of people in the world: men, women and ministers. The latter, by this definition, are sexless, sinless entities more filled with Spirit than spirits who go through life with blinders that shield them from all the vicissitudes of worldly struggles...It's unreal–but that's his job description: unreal.

There is no other job on earth that expects a man to work every possible waking moment, to comfort the sick and dying, to be the tower of strength for the bereaved and/or the anxious bridegroom, to counsel the maritally afflicted, to pray at a moment's notice, to be all-wise in the problems of child care and in-family jousting, to administer a [large] budget, to raise money for loan payments without issuing bonds, to run a church program efficiently with an all-volunteer staff that serves when it feels like it, to act as building and grounds maintenance supervisor, to prepare miraculously and preach eloquently, to dress meticulously but not too well, to be a saint in all interpersonal relationships with language that even your grandmother couldn't question, to love his children and see that they are raised in an exemplary manner, to keep his own marriage and personal habits above question, to be never grossly (or netly, either) in debt, and to set a pattern of living that all can follow in personal faith and spiritual development. In case you have forgotten what I am talking about, the above is the job description in abbreviated form for the twentieth-century Man of God, commonly known as minister.[7]

The difference between the exalted view of the office and the daily reality of pastoral life can be striking. Here is one way of looking at it.

One pastor said, "The goals of my ministry are the salvation of mankind and the coming of God's kingdom on this earth." When reciting his accomplishments on the way to achieving these goals, he boasted, "We have blacktopped the parking lot of the church and redecorated the inside of the parsonage from top to bottom."[8]

Among respondents to our survey, 47% indicated that unwritten congregational expectations contributed to their decision to resign.[9] Too many of us load too much baggage onto the office of pastorate, effectively placing pastors in the position of God. Paul's view of ministry is much more attractive. "But we have this treasure in jars of clay to show that this all-surpassing power is from God and not from us" (2 Cor. 4:7).

Unique Leadership

A pastor must lead, but he is not a boss. He is responsible for what happens, but he has no authority beyond his ability to persuade. A tricky balance. Peter described this balance as "not lording it over those entrusted to you, but being examples to the flock" (1 Pet. 5:3). With characteristic directness Chuck Swindoll says, "[Leadership is] influence."[10] In practical terms, this means that a pastor cannot manage in the same way other managers do. He cannot simply say, "Here is the plan, let's do it." His world is more complicated than that. He must win over the board. He must consider the feelings of the opinion leaders among the congregation. He must figure out a way around the omnipresent church crank. His is a volunteer organization.

His congregation has hired him to lead, but they are not always in the mood to follow. The people in the pew have their own ideas and are often unwilling to part with them. Thus, in making decisions and implementing programs, a pastor has to carefully consider whether or not the people are with him. His leadership, in order to be effective, must be "participatory."[11] This kind of leadership is an art form.

Unique Accountability

In business, workers are necessarily accountable to someone. The CEO of any company has the greatest accountability of all. He or she must answer to the board, the stockholders and, ultimately, the customers. If a CEO is fortunate, the board will clearly define how it will supervise and evaluate his or her performance.

The pastor is not so fortunate. In one sense he has a clear accountability. "Not many of you should presume to be teachers my brothers because you know that we who teach will be judged more strictly" (James 3:1). This verse spells out clearly that one who teaches the Word of God is accountable to God, period. However, a pastor quickly discovers that his biblical accountability to God can be compromised by the temptation to please people.

The average church expects a pastor to be accountable to two groups of people. His accountability covers a broad and sometimes unpredictable range of issues.

He is accountable to the church board. Noted author Bobb Biehl argues strenuously for the accountability of the "senior executive" of any Christian organization to the leadership board: "The cruelest response you can make as a board member is to 'let it slide' when you see a senior executive struggling."[12] Accountability of leaders one to another is an important biblical mandate, especially in moral matters. "Do not entertain an accusation against an elder unless it is brought by two or three witnesses. Those who sin are to be rebuked publicly so that others may take warning" (1 Tim. 5:19-20). In modern churches the exact nature of the pastor's accountability to the board varies from church to church. However, it generally focuses on his role as a leader. The board deals with the programs and problems of the church. As the "senior executive," the pastor is accountable to the board for any area in which both he and the board are involved. For example, if the board is hearing from members of the congregation that they do not wish to "greet one another" during the service, the pastor is going to hear about it. If giving or attendance is down, the board will give attention to what the pastor can and should do about it. The pastor discusses his ideas with the board in hopes of gaining their input and often their approval. This provides for a measure of accountability for performance on the job.

He is also accountable to the church body at large. These people pay his salary and choose every week whether or not to show up. Further, some within the congregation take it upon themselves to be pastoral watchdogs. The pastor may be held accountable for anything (professional or personal) that suits the individual observer. Since the expectations within a given congregation vary widely, this type of accountability is unpredictable. It also has significant implications, particularly for a first-time pastor.

Frequently expressed negatively, this kind of "accountability" can have a telling effect. Stan Fedders, a pastoral veteran, recalls an early experience with a pastoral watchdog. His church had decided to purchase artificial plants for the front of the auditorium. It was difficult to arrange them attractively because of the presence of the Christian and American flags on the platform. The flags and greenery just didn't fit together. So Stan took down the flags. To at least one member of the congregation, this was a grievous and possibly a malicious mistake. He exerted pressure until Stan relented and put the flags back up.

Earl Phillips, an ex-pastor, offended a church member by mowing the lawn of the parsonage with his shirt off. To his amazement, it became a significant issue. He never did it again. Russ Rassmussen's decision to grow a beard touched off a controversy that resulted in the loss of two member families.

Often overlooked but most important, we are shaped by what people expect of us, especially in the first pastorate. One study by Drew University Theological School of its recent graduates concluded that the primary task of the first five years of ministry seemed to be "to acquire the self-image of being a professional capable of providing the services a congregation declares it needs from its minister." Rather than fulfilling their own sense of calling, fledgling pastors usually try to satisfy the expectations of their congregations.[13]

The accountability of a pastor to both church board and body is unequaled in that it covers his professional as well as his private affairs. His family has legitimate needs and the pastor is accountable to the church and its leadership for his involvement and effectiveness at home. This is biblical. Paul told Timothy that a man aspiring to the office of overseer must "manage his own family well and see that his children obey him with proper respect" (1 Tim. 3:4). He adds that if a man can't manage his home, he is incapable of managing a church (1 Tim. 3:5). His advice to Titus was similar: "An elder must be blameless, the husband of but one wife, a man whose children believe and are not open to the charge of being wild and disobedient" (Titus 1:6).

"Wild and disobedient children," writes Alexander Strauch, "are a bad reflection on the home, especially on the father's lack of discipline and inability to guide others. If one who aspires to eldership lacks such ability, he will never be able to manage God's family."[14] In a very real sense, a pastor's family life is part of his job. His calling demands accountability for more than just the performance of his assigned duties. He is biblically accountable for the management of his home life.

Since churches have a notorious lack of respect for a pastor's private time, a pastor must actively fend off members of his congregation in order to carve out some time for family life. More than a few pastors have found that in order to have uninterrupted family time, they must leave town. Excess demands on a pastor's time tend to place him in an awkward position. In order to fulfill one set of expectations by the people (that of spiritually healthy wife and children), he has to deliberately frustrate a different set of expectations (that of an omnipresent and continually available pastor).

In addition to the tension between the needs of the church and those of his family, the pastor faces varying expectations within the church body itself. Older people usually prefer a "country parson" who spends a lot of his time visiting. Younger families often want a "full-service church"[15] headed by a competent manager. These expectations can be especially difficult for pastors because of the tendency to measure their personal spiritual worth by their performance in the ministry.

Tony (chapter 1) experienced this phenomenon firsthand. His ministry in an older church required that he spend lots of time with long-time members. On the other hand, younger members constantly reminded him of the need for children's programming–programming which the church "pillars" found frivolous. Conflict developed over time and priorities. Tony was accountable to both the older and younger groups. The fact that he couldn't satisfy both groups contributed to his burnout.

Sadly, while he had no shortage of "bosses," meaningful accountability was absent. No one made sure Tony was maintaining his spiritual disciplines, getting enough rest and exercise, or resolving his frustration over the difficulty of his ministry. Such accountability might have made a difference. Simply having someone care that much would have been an enormous encouragement.

Many church boards expect the pastor to keep all of the people more or less happy and lead the church to new spiritual heights at the same time! Yeah, right. This is an impossible task and every pastor knows it. But a pastor ignores these conflicting demands only at his own risk. His ministerial well-being, his future, and his paycheck all rest on the good will of these well-intentioned but sometimes fickle people. With these and many more conflicting and sometimes unreasonable pressures, a pastor can be tempted to lead an unbalanced life, to ignore spiritual disciplines, to forego rest and exercise, and to let vital relationships run on autopilot while he tries to please people.

Paul urged Timothy to set the pace for the church rather than be shaped by expectations. "Be diligent in these matters; give yourself wholly to them, so that everyone may see your progress. Watch your life and doctrine closely. Persevere in them, because if you do, you will save both yourself and your hearers" (1 Tim. 4:15-16). "Preach the Word; be prepared in season and out of season; correct, rebuke, and encourage–with great patience and careful instruction" (2 Tim. 4:2). To be a people pleaser is to abdicate the leadership role intended for pastors. Nevertheless, many pastors face regular pressure to do just that.

The real irony is that while pastors have many demands, there is little supervision in the disciplines most likely to make or break a man's ministry. He works alone and often no one knows what he does with his time. How productive is he? Is he growing in his abilities? How is his attitude? Our survey indicated that in eleven critical areas there is little or no accountability for pastors. These included use of time, various spiritual disciplines, family relationships, financial responsibility, and continuing education. Only 27% of pastors surveyed were held accountable in any of the areas listed. Nearly one out of four cited poor accountability as a contributing factor in their decision to resign.[16]

Many studies indicate that as a group pastors are not faring well spiritually or domestically. A Leadership survey found that 81% of pastors feel they spend too little time with their mate. The same survey revealed a whole spectrum of specific marital troubles among pastors ranging from communication difficulties to physical abuse. Only slightly more than half considered pastoral ministry beneficial to home life.[17]

An earlier survey found that 37% of pastors responding had experienced inappropriate sexual contact outside of their marriage.[18] This demonstrates (among other things) the truth that while they have many notions of what a pastor should be and do, churches frequently offer ineffective or misplaced accountability. There are lots of bosses, but little supervision.

Unique Salary

What makes a pastor's salary package unique is not that it is low, but that it is low in comparison to other professions requiring advanced training and heavy responsibilities.

George Barna points out that experience and education along with the size of a church do make a difference in the average salary of a pastor. However, it tends to be "substantially less than the average salaries paid to other highly trained and experienced professionals such as teachers, corporate managers, engineers and doctors."[19]

This discrepancy is a result of several factors. Salaries are often set by an exhausted board toward the end of a long business meeting. In addition, the people who pass on the salary of a pastor usually compare it with their own, not realizing that the figure listed in the church budget represents more than the actual paycheck.[20] Lack of material compensation is one significant way in which the congregation communicates lack of approval. Inadequate compensation says to a pastor that while his people expect much of him, they don't really value him.

Because of his unique role, your pastor often feels alone in a church full of people. Your understanding and positive response lessens the strain considerably. In a church where Bob served, one lady consistently wrote encouragement cards to him. A couple of times a month he could count on getting these statements of affirmation. She didn't pretend to understand all that his job entailed. She just said that she thanked God for him, had been blessed by the sermon, appreciated his gentleness with his children, and so on. These encouraging words were rays of light often restoring perspective that Bob had lost in the press of church affairs. She was a Barnabas to him.

Every pastor needs one of those. Such people make the uniqueness of the pastorate a source of joy rather than pain. If you can similarly affirm your pastor you will help him know that, while his career is unique, he definitely has a real job.

You Can Help!

With the exception of the unique calling, all of the issues in this chapter will be discussed more fully later in the book. For each subject, we will offer specific steps a church member can take to help his pastor deal with that issue. For now, we simply want to recommend that you recognize the uniqueness of his job. In the coming weeks, months, and years encourage your pastor in practical ways such as:

1. Stop comparing the pastor's job to yours.

The responsibilities, hours, accountability, corporate dynamics, and even salary structure are probably so different from your own that to compare them is to compare apples and oranges. Comparisons are frequently thinly veiled criticisms. They invariably miss the mark.

2. Affirm the value of your pastor's work.

Today's society destroys many pastors self-esteem. In the past, pastors were often the most respected members of a community; today they often wonder if their work honestly helps people. Let your pastor know that you are not just waiting for him to slip up, that you are on his team and are planning to stay there. Rejuvenate his energy by sending him notes to express specific instances when his ministry has built your faith.

3. Offer your assistance.

Schedule a meeting with your pastor in his office or over breakfast or lunch. Once you've finished the initial small talk, look your pastor in the eye and say, "Pastor, how can I help you?" Seriously offer him your support, not just your suggestions, and be ready to roll up your sleeves and work side-by-side with him.

4. Boost his dreams and hopes for the church.

Listen to your pastor's hopes and dreams for the church, his ministry, and family. Explore opportunities and methods to help him make dreams become a reality. Do whatever it takes to help him make things happen.

5. Start a Pastor's Prayer Team.

He is in a demanding and often dangerous place. The enemy has marked him for destruction. Your prayers can shield him from more than you know. Organize a team of seven people who will covenant to pray for the pastor once a week. Or, if you have enough committed people, bring together 30 people who will agree to pray once a month for the pastor. On Sunday mornings, members of the Pastor's Prayer Team can take turns meeting with the pastor before church to pray with him for the Sunday services.

–End Chapter Two–

[1]John Bradley and Jay Carty with Russ Korth, Unlocking Your Sixth Suitcase: How to Love What You Do and Do What You Love (Colorado Springs, CO: NavPress, Navigators, 1991), 31.

[2]Edward B. Bratcher, The Walk-On-Water Syndrome: Dealing with Professional Hazards in the Ministry, with a foreword by Wayne Oates (Waco, TX: Word Books, Word, Inc., 1984), 73.

[3]Pastoral Survey, see appendix.

[4]Bratcher, The Walk-On-Water Syndrome, 69.

[5]Bratcher, The Walk-On-Water Syndrome, 70-71.

[6]Wilson T. Hogue, Homiletics and Pastoral Theology (Winona Lake, IN: Free Methodist Publishing House, 1946), 252-253; quoted in Charles U. Wagner, The Pastor: His Life and Work (Schaumburg, IL: Regular Baptist Press, 1976), 13.

[7]Ruth Truman, Underground Manual For Ministers' Wives (And Other Bewildered Women) (Nashville, TN: Abingdon Press, 1974), 26.

[8]Nathaneal M. Guptill, How to Be a Pastor in a Mad, Mad World (St. Louis: Bethany Press, 1970), 21-22; quoted in Bratcher, The Walk-On-Water Syndrome, 138.

[9]Pastoral Survey, see appendix.

[10]Chuck Swindoll, Leadership: Influence That Inspires, Lifemaps (Waco, TX: Word Books, Word, Inc., 1985), 19.

[11]Kennon L. Callahan, Twelve Keys to an Effective Church: Strategic Planning for Mission (San Francisco: Harper & Row, Publishers, 1983), 55.

[12]Bobb Biehl and Ted W. Engstrom, Increasing Your Boardroom Confidence (Sisters, OR: Questar Publishing, 1988), 196.

[13]Richard P. Hansen, "The Sound of Clashing Expectations," Leadership Journal 5, no. 3 (Summer 1984): 78-79.

[14]Alexander Strauch, Biblical Eldership: An Urgent Call to Restore Biblical Church Leadership, 2d ed. (Littleton, CO: Lewis & Roth Publishers, 1988), 174.

[15]Gary McIntosh, "The Blended Church," Handout: Model #2, in class notes, from lecture, "Understanding Baby Boomers," presented in "Min 801, Pastors' Symposium, Contemporary Models of Ministry: Reaching Baby Boomers," 15-19 October 1990, Talbot School of Theology, Biola University, La Mirada, CA.

[16]Pastoral Survey, see appendix.

17David Goetz, "Is the Pastor's Family Safe at Home?" <u>Leadership Journal</u> 13, no. 4 (Fall 1992): 38-44.

18Richard A. Blackmon, "Survey of Pastors," in "The Hazards of the Ministry," Psy.D. diss., Graduate School of Psychology, Fuller Theological Seminary, Pasadena, CA, 1984.

19George Barna, <u>Today's Pastors: A Revealing Look at What Pastors Are Saying about Themselves, Their Peers and the Pressures They Face</u> (Ventura, CA: Regal Books, Gospel Light, 1993), 37.

20Larry W. Osborne, "Negotiating a Fair Salary," <u>Leadership Journal</u> 8, no. 1 (Winter 1987): 86-88.

Chapter Three

They Taught Us Everything But How To Run A Church

"IF ONLY I HAD RECEIVED better training, I could have done a better job." Fred had always felt insecure about his education. He had supported his family as a warehouseman while he earned undergraduate and master's degrees in theology. Along the way he gained some small practical experience as an intern in his church.

Upon graduation, Fred was called to pastor a church in a town a few miles from his home. His biggest question was, "Will they show up again after the first week?" Fred discovered that the daily realities of ministry included large doses of conflict management, crisis counseling, and administration. He began to feel overwhelmed. He had little or no training in these areas. He found himself chairing board meetings, planning funerals, and setting budget priorities. He was unprepared for any of it. There had been no courses in seminary dealing with domestic violence or other crises that pastors face. The reality of church conflict had been taught, but no practical approaches to managing conflict had been offered.

There was an often-voiced assumption on the part of his seminary mentors that because the pastoral epistles deal with substantive and practical issues, a student simply needed to learn their principles to be prepared for local church ministry. Fred needed more. He needed guidance in the practical application of those principles in a real ministry setting. His lack of practical expertise left him insecure about his ability to lead. His uncertainty grew with gradual exposure to the realities of ministry. It dogged him through nearly a decade of ministry and was a significant factor in his decision to leave the ministry for secular employment. Fred is not alone. The truth is none of us learned *everything* we need to know and many of us learned everything *but* how to run a church.

Inadequate training is a significant problem for many of today's pastors.

They enter ministry only to discover that their seminary education didn't equip them as well as they had hoped. They find themselves "behind the curve," struggling both to discard what no longer works and to learn what does. Some even consider a career change as a result.

The World of Seminary

The average pastor in America today has more education than pastors of any other generation in American history. Over half of the pastors participating in our survey hold master's degrees, yet 60% indicated that they feel inadequately trained. How can this be? The answer lies in the nature of seminary education.

Many needed pastoral skills are not taught in curriculum. Courses in church finance, time management, group dynamics, counseling, and numerous other practical subjects would help equip pastors for their work. However, laying a solid theological foundation for ministry takes precedence over such practical issues in the world of seminary. This is as it should be. A seminary is by definition "an environment in which something originates *and from which it is propagated*".[1] This is the key to understanding the world of the seminary. A seminary is charged with the dual responsibilities of *training* ministers and at the same time *preserving and propagating* the basics of the faith along with the theological perspectives of whatever heritage(s) it serves. Dallas Theological Seminary states these dual commitments early on in its catalog:

> The mission of Dallas Theological Seminary as a professional, graduate-level school is to prepare men and women for ministry as godly servant-leaders in the body of Christ worldwide ...

> Dallas Seminary stands unequivocally committed to the Scriptures, God's inerrant, infallible, authoritative written revelation. Members of the school's boards and faculty subscribe to the Seminary's Doctrinal Statement, which is distinctively complete and detailed, thus helping safeguard its unswerving theological stance since the school's founding over 70 years ago.[2]

While seminaries vary in theology and perspective, similar statements of commitment to training and adherence to theological moorings figure prominently in most catalogs.

The world of seminary is by its very nature resistant to change. It is important that it be so. Seminaries do not exist to promote change, but to preserve truth. The world of seminary is also a world of the academic—a world in which theory and philosophy are central. Again, this is necessary to its function. As we shall see, these two necessary truths mean that adequate education for modern pastors requires a new model—one that stresses lifelong education.

A World that Resists Change

Once in the not-too-distant past, a seminary could count on sending a graduate out to minister in a church environment very much like the one in which he grew up. He had already learned the realities of church life in church. Seminary gave him the theological expertise necessary to lead that church. Those days are gone.

In the past half-century, America has undergone technological and social change at a breathtaking rate. In this brief span of time, America has moved from an industrial to an information-based economy.[3] Until 1956 the majority of the work force labored at blue collar occupations; today 60-70% hold information-related jobs and only 13% hold manufacturing jobs. At the turn of the century, fully one-third of America's work force earned a living in farming. Today the number is less than 3%.[4]

Not only has the way we earn a living changed, we have witnessed an unprecedented shift in our society's basic values. Baby boomers, as members of the post-World War II generation are called, view life differently from their parents in virtually every area. They spend more and save less. They question authority and change careers, marriages, and churches more often than their parents ever did. In these and other ways, baby boomers represent a whole new culture. Preliminary evaluations seem to indicate that children of baby boomers are as different from their parents as boomers are from theirs.[5] These generational changes mean that today's pastor ministers in a multi-cultural environment with varying and often conflicting demands. What works with part of the church doesn't work with all.

A seminary graduate can no longer count on ministering in the same ecclesiastical environment in which he grew up. An old mentor voiced his opinion that young men entering ministry have it tougher than when he started. To our amazement he said, "I was in the pastorate for fifteen years before I was ever called upon to deal with the issue of divorce. I was in it for thirty years before music in the church

43

became a divisive issue." Since that conversation, another fifteen years have passed and the world is a different place—again.

If a pastor looks to his seminary for help in adjusting to these new realities, he often looks in vain. While his seminary education equipped him to remain true to the faith, chances are it did not equip him to communicate that faith effectively in today's changing world.

Seminaries do not exist to promote timely methodology, but to preserve timeless theology. Because of their very nature, seminaries distrust and resist change. They exist to graduate ministers grounded in never-changing biblical principles, and tend to view any change affecting church life with a certain degree of suspicion. New practices often have theological implications. For example, church growth experts urge pastors to "preach to felt needs."[6] In a few instances, pastors practicing this principle may move away from the most central truths of the gospel or even away from substantive biblical exposition entirely. When that occurs, biblical content is sacrificed on the altar of practicality. Since the proclamation of the Word of God is central to the church's purpose for existence, seminaries are right to carefully scrutinize any practice that might compromise this function. As one seminary professor put it, "Everything we do should be based on the Bible. The Bible is very practical."[7] His statement agrees with those of Scripture, especially as they relate to preaching.

> Preach the Word; be prepared in season and out of season; correct, rebuke and encourage—with great patience and careful instruction. For the time will come when men will not put up with sound doctrine. Instead, to suit their own desires, they will gather around them a great number of teachers to say what their itching ears want to hear (2 Tim. 4:2-3).

Sadly, the church is not immune to fads or famous personalities. Some of what captures the church's fancy is potentially destructive. Seminaries are justifiably skeptical of change but, because of this, it takes time for theological educators to pass judgment on new methods. The result is that in preserving the theology of our fathers, many seminaries also preserve the methodology of our fathers.

> Gary Collins, a professor of counseling at Trinity Evangelical Divinity School, was concerned that those entering the ministry "know the biblical, theological world, but they don't know the

real world in which we live. We're living in a Corinthian age, but we're preparing students for the Victorian age."[8]

This "behind-the-curve" facet of seminary life is one reason many pastors find themselves struggling with the realities of modern church life. They often have advanced degrees, but are poorly equipped either to lead a culturally diverse church or to express Christianity in terms a changed world can understand. An institution that teaches and guards doctrinal truths and therefore is properly skeptical of change is not the place to look for cutting edge methodology.

A World of the Academic

The world of seminary also tends toward the academic rather than the practical. Writing in *Leadership*, William Willimon observes:

> Seminary professors, caught between the demands of the academy and the values of the church, have usually pleased the academy. The academy, with its values of academic elitism, pursuit of intellectual minutiae, and presumed scholarly objectivity, has become the credentialing agency for seminary faculty—to the detriment of the congregation.[9]

Imagine a doctor with all the necessary academic credentials to practice medicine. He earned straight A's in anatomy, booked through biochemistry, and was phenomenal in pharmacology. There is just one hitch. When he set up his own practice, he suddenly realized that he had never actually treated a patient, made a diagnosis, stitched a wound, or written a prescription. Ridiculous! Although his education in medical knowledge may have been outstanding, his training was grossly inadequate. He would not yet be competent to practice medicine. Imagine that doctor ten years later, having learned by experience much of what he missed in school. Would he be well equipped? No. During those ten years, medical knowledge doubled and doubled again.[10] While he worked to catch up, the world did not wait for him. Though he may have developed a solid foundation in medical knowledge and skill, he would still be years behind the cutting edge in medicine.

Pastors find themselves in a similar position. They have learned much in seminary but lack hands-on training under the supervision of seasoned practitioners of the pastoral art. They lack expertise when it comes to translating theology into practice. They find themselves in over their heads when it comes to common pastoral functions such as marriage counseling, leadership development, practical discipleship, or assimilating new members.

Looking at the church is a bit like looking at seminary in a mirror. One sees the same elements, but in opposite proportions. If a seminary emphasizes languages first, followed by theology, biblical exposition, and practicum, a church emphasizes these elements in reverse. Practical matters absorb the bulk of time and attention, followed by biblical exposition, and theology. Languages come in a distant last.

Of course theology and philosophy are important. They are the essential framework that keeps ministry in perspective and true to its purpose. However, a pastor spends the bulk of his time applying theology to real situations. In daily church life, a pastor's attentions are taken up with more mundane controversies than the Reformation. He is dealing with feuding deaconesses, three-hour board meetings, and an endless tug-of-war over worship styles. Budgets and bulletins occupy his mind more than Bultmann or Barth. Through it all, he tries to figure out how to motivate his flock to reach its community (let alone the world) for Christ. For this he needs more than academic theology.

When a pastor deals with a suicidal person, he needs more than a treatise on anthropology or the redemptive model. Theology helps the pastor to understand the true dynamics of this situation, but he needs to know how to talk to this person. There is a need for the practicality of Christ's model of discipleship. Jesus taught his disciples by allowing them to experience ministry alongside him. As they watched and occasionally took part, Jesus applied theological truths to real-life situations. Thus, instead of taking notes on a lecture about the nature of faith, the disciples watched one of their own walk on the water (Matt. 14:29). Instead of yawning through assigned reading on the methodology of cross-cultural missions, the disciples were present when Jesus evangelized a Samaritan woman (John 4:4-42). Instead of writing a research paper on legalism, the disciples experienced the continual friction between Jesus and the Pharisees. This model of discipleship emphasized answers to questions like "How?" and "Why?"

This kind of front-line approach is somewhat foreign to the academic atmosphere of seminary. This is not necessarily bad. Some argue persuasively that the academic nature of seminary education is necessary and good—that an understanding of theology and philosophy is all that seminaries were designed to offer. One denominational official responded to a complaint from a seminary student about the "theoretical nature" of theological education.

> We are not sending you here to take nuts-and-bolts courses or to get practical experience in parish life ... You will spend a lifetime in continuing your education on a practical plane, and we can always establish workshops to address specific needs or deficiencies as they arise. We send you to seminary for three years to get what you will really need to begin your ministry—the broad, biblical, historical, and theological background for ministry in the church today. If you aren't getting that by shunning those courses, then the problem is not with the seminary, but with you.[11]

Perhaps here we see the essential problem. School is school, and church is church. It is difficult for a seminary to prepare an individual for all that he will face in church. Only church can do that. The seminary can only provide a foundation on which to build. Seminaries that attempt to bridge the chasm between theoretical theological courses and practical ministry often fall short. Willimon wrote that, in his own experience, the so-called "practical courses," based as they were on urban ministry, often taught him things that were utterly useless in his rural parish.[12] Many pastors have been taught similarly useless methodologies.

The fact remains that a church needs more than academic excellence in a seminary graduate. It needs a pastor who can deal with practical realities like conflict management and counseling. Often, young pastors come into church ministry ready to answer questions that no one is asking. The questions on the minds of churchgoers have little to do with ancient theological controversies, the tenses of Greek verbs, or the relative strengths and weaknesses of the Textus Receptus. These things have an important place in the pastor's training, but they don't cross the bridge to where the congregation lives. Billy Graham cited an example of a church that set up two stipulations in its search for a pastor. "One, they did not want a seminary graduate; two, they wanted no one who had taken Greek."[13]

In recent years a more balanced approach has emerged in the world of the seminary, an approach that integrates theory and practicum, academic integrity, and hands-on practicality. This can be seen in the course offerings of many major seminaries. Talbot School of Theology offers a healthy emphasis on "Field Education" and "Field Internship."[14]

In their M.Div. program, Trinity Evangelical Divinity School offers an emphasis on Christianity and contemporary culture. There is also a requirement for field education for all M.Div. students.[15] As part of their philosophy of educational integration, Asbury Theological Seminary offers courses in "Supervised Ministry."[16]

While such programs are not new, they are receiving greater emphasis today. Some mega-churches such as Overlake Christian Church in Kirkland, Wash.,[17] and Grace Community Church in Sun Valley, Calif.,[18] offer practical training for leaders by operating their own seminaries. More recently Denver Seminary explored the idea of conducting some of a seminary student's education at satellite training centers connected to the main campus hub. Centers for church planting, urban, suburban, and rural ministry training are a few of the centers that may be developed in the coming years.

These efforts to wed practical experience with the theological disciplines are very encouraging in view of scriptural directives. "And the things you have heard me say in the presence of many witnesses, entrust to reliable men who will also be qualified to teach others" (2 Tim. 2:2). Paul's method of reproducing leaders certainly included a balance between deep theological truth and practical experience. He taught others the pastoral craft by working alongside of them in ministry. Nowhere is this clearer than in his recruitment and subsequent training of Timothy (Acts 16:1-3, et al.). Our Lord demonstrated similar balance when He sent His disciples out two by two (Luke 10). It may be that we are on our way to solving this dichotomy between the world of the seminary and that of the church.

However, many pastors now face problems and opportunities in a rapidly changing environment for which they are unprepared. They entered ministry believing that they had learned what they would need only to discover that the learning had just begun. Sixty percent of the pastors and ex-pastors we surveyed indicated that their training was inadequate. Of those, 17% cited inadequate training as a factor in their decision to resign.[19] These men were trained in theology but ill-equipped for ministry. For some of them, the shortcomings of their education were fatal to their careers as pastors.

A World in Need of a New Model

Upgrading seminary degree programs is helpful, but we are convinced that what we need is a whole new way of looking at theological education. We tend to expect from seminaries something that no institution can offer; namely, an education adequate for a lifetime of ministry. As we have seen, seminaries exist to preserve and teach doctrine. They are therefore both skeptical of change and academic in approach. While many seminaries could make their course offerings more practical, this provides limited benefits since continual change quickly makes methods obsolete. It is time for pastors and seminaries alike to realize that a theological education alone at the beginning of a pastor's career will not equip him for decades of pastoral service. Instead, we must accept the reality that effective education is that which continues *for the duration of a pastor's ministry.*

Edward B. Bratcher writes:

For many years it was assumed that basic seminary training provided skills to carry one through his whole ministry. This was the view when I graduated some thirty years ago. Today it is recognized by both educators and ministers that education for ministry must span the whole career. This approach is made imperative by the rapid and radical changes in the forms and context of ministry.[20]

Because of today's rapid pace of change, an effective pastor has to continually update his skills. For example, cold turkey calling, a time-honored method of outreach, is no longer effective in many areas due to people's reluctance to open their doors for strangers.[21] There are new ways to reach out through direct mail, telemarketing, special events, or ministries directed at common needs. A pastor's ability to lead a church in effective outreach today is therefore dependent upon his ability to learn what works here and now within the parameters of Scripture to accomplish his purpose.

The Apostle Paul modeled adaptability. When his preaching in the synagogue ceased to be effective, he began to hold discussions in a lecture hall owned by a philosopher named Tyrannus (Acts 19:8-10). When he visited Athens, he taught the philosophers on Mars Hill about the identity of their "unknown God" (Acts 17:23). He spoke openly about his methodological flexibility. "I have become all things to all men so that by all possible means I might save some" (1 Cor. 9:22). He knew how to adjust to a changing situation or a different culture without compromising his message.

In today's fast-paced world, pastors need such knowledge. They must accept the modern maxim that apart from the truths of Scripture "the only constant is the slow drip of constant change."[22] Adjusting for continual change requires a pastor to be continually learning. This is precisely what a conventional seminary education cannot do for him. In a world in which knowledge doubles every five years,[23] a pastor cannot rely on the methodology he learned in seminary. Continuing education is not just a luxury but a necessity for the effective pastor. Without it, he will rely on an education that suited him to minister in a world that no longer exists.

The world of the seminary is already engaged in a paradigm shift away from a "front-end-only" model, toward a "lifelong" model of education. In 1984, Leonard Sweet wrote of a rapid shift taking place in the world of theological education centering on continuing education.

> The amazing speed with which slow-moving theological institutions within this past decade established D.Min. degrees and continuing education programs is solid evidence of an attempt to reconnect pastors with seminaries. The support for the local congregation has become a diapason of seminary life. Not since the nineteenth century has there been such a widespread movement to bring theological curricula into significant conversation with congregational life.[24]

The doctorate of ministry is a professional degree program designed to be completed by a pastor *while he is involved in ministry*. This involves relatively short periods of formal classroom instruction along with much individual research and practical application. Its emphasis is clearly on the practical aspects of church ministry such as church administration, small groups, contemporary biblical preaching, contemporary models of ministry, and church growth. In 1969 there were seven such programs. Today approximately 100 schools offer the degree.[25] This is laudable. However, a sobering fact remains. Only about 10% of today's pastors have doctoral degrees—not all of them are the practical doctorate of ministry.[26]

The D.Min. formula of small amounts of academic isolation mixed with large amounts of direct involvement in church ministry is an effective combination. The ongoing popularity of professional seminars dealing with the methodology of ministry is evidence of the need pastor's feel in this area.

In today's world, a seminary graduate should expect to maintain a life-long relationship with the seminary, not just as an alumnus, but as a student.

Many of the shortcomings of a seminary education seem to be unavoidable. Seminaries are resistant to change, but this is a necessary part of their function. They act as theological anchors helping the church to avoid being "blown here and there by every wind of teaching" (Eph. 4:14). Seminaries deal heavily with academic theory and less with practicum, but this too is part of their function. Pastors need the theological moorings provided by seminary to enable them to remain biblical in the midst of change. A seminary education that is heavy in methodology, however, becomes obsolete in a short time.

The answer to this problem lies in a new model for theological education, one that stresses changeless theology as a foundation and changing methodology as a way of building on that foundation. The latter must take place over a lifetime.

Pastors cannot be content with what they already know. They must always be learning. For this they need the support of their church. This is one area where pastors and their churches need to make a steadfast effort knowing that in due season they will reap a reward if they don't give up (1 Cor. 15:58, Gal. 6:9).

You Can Help!

The "behind-the-curve" approach to ministry need not be the case in your church. There are many ways you can help. Here are some suggestions.

1. Encourage or require your pastor to continue his education.

This can take the form of seminars, or an advanced degree like the doctorate of ministry designed to develop proficiency in some area of ministry. Periodic "time-out" experiences in which a pastor learns in a different environment may offer the best educational experiences of his life. The first course in my D.Min. program was a pastor's symposium on contemporary models of ministry. It dealt with the differences between generations and focused on ways of reaching baby boomers. I had been groping for answers in those areas. The subject was so relevant to me that I took ten pages of notes per day. Because of the brief and intense period of instruction sandwiched between longer periods of reading and hands-on application, I learned more from that class than from any previous course. The mental stimulation alone gained from such a course can be as important as the material learned. One reason this approach is so effective is that the pastor sees the importance of what he is learning. He can come right home and apply it in his ministry. This makes the experience valuable for him as well as for the church.

Of course, there is a price to pay. Your pastor will need the time off to take the training. The church must also make continuing education a priority in its budget. It will be worth it. In my view, it is not just for the sake of its pastor that a church should do this, but for the sake of the church itself. Rightly considered, education is more than an expense. It is an investment, one that will return to the church through the efforts of a better equipped pastor.

2. Start an internship program for theological students in your church.

Internships represent a biblical model for learning the work of the ministry. They acquaint a student "preacher" with the realities of ministry and advance the work of the church at the same time. As noted earlier, more pastors fail as a result of poor leadership skills than as a result of theological heresy. A well-run internship can give a future minister an "inside look" that will prove invaluable. It's a little like pilot training. After a requisite number of hours with the instructor by his side, the student will be ready to "fly solo."

An additional benefit involved with internship ministries is that the practical experience allows a student to learn more effectively from his formal theological education. A person learns more effectively when he understands from experience the relevance of the material he is studying.

3. Be patient with a young pastor as he learns the many things that he can only learn through hard experience.

In fact, be more than patient. Be encouraging. Your pastor has his share of critics. While he always needs input, he needs to know you are in his corner. The early years of ministry can be formative for a pastor. Make sure you encourage him during these years. A truth that applies to pastors as much as anyone else is that good judgment comes from experience and experience comes from bad judgment. In my judgment, a little encouragement and a lot of learning can keep a man hanging in there through all the painful Mondays.

–End Chapter Three–

[1]Merriam Webster's Collegiate Dictionary, 10th ed., s.v. "seminary."

[2]"Dallas Theological Seminary: 1995-96, Catalog," Dallas, TX, 10.

[3]For further information see Gary L. McIntosh and Glen S. Martin The Issachar Factor (Nashville: Broadman & Holman, 1993).

[4]John Naisbitt, Megatrends: Ten New Directions Transforming Our Lives (New York: Warner Books, 1982), 12-14.

[5]Gary L. McIntosh, "Understanding Baby Boomers," lecture presented in "Min 801, Pastors' Symposium, Contemporary Models of Ministry: Reaching Baby Boomers," 15-19 October 1990, Talbot School of Theology, Biola University, La Mirada, CA, class notes, 1.

[6]Don Sunukjian, lecture presented in "Min 810: Contemporary Biblical Preaching," 11-15 May 1992, Talbot School of Theology, Biola University, La Mirada, CA.

[7]Taken from editorial comments on this chapter by William F. Edmondson, professor of practical theology at Faith Baptist Bible College, Ankeny, IA.

[8]"Special Report: How Common is Pastoral Indiscretion?" Leadership Journal 9, no. 1 (Winter 1988): 12.

[9]William Willimon, responding to Leonard I. Sweet, "Seminary and Congregation: A Lovers' Quarrel?" Leadership Journal 5, no. 3 (Summer 1984): 108.

[10]McIntosh, "Understanding Baby Boomers," class notes, 2.

[11]Sweet, "Seminary and Congregation," 107-108.

[12]Willimon, responding to Sweet, "Seminary and Congregation," 108.

[13]Billy Graham; quoted in David McKenna, responding to Sweet, "Seminary and Congregation," 110.

[14]"Talbot School of Theology, Graduate Program: 1994-95," Talbot School of Theology, Biola University, La Mirada, CA, T-5.

[15]"Trinity Evangelical Divinity School: 1994-95 Catalog and Application," Deerfield, IL, 73-74.

[16]"Asbury Theological Seminary: 1994-1996 Catalog," Wilmore, KY, 31-36.

[17]"Overlake School of the Ministry," 1st ed., Catalog, Overlake Christian School of Ministry, Kirkland, WA.

[18]"The Master's Seminary: 1994/96 Catalog," The Master's Seminary, Sun Valley, CA, 12.

[19]Pastoral Survey, see appendix.

[20]Edward B. Bratcher, The Walk-On-Water Syndrome: Dealing with Professional Hazards in the Ministry, with a foreword by Wayne Oates (Waco, TX: Word Books, Word, Inc.), 162.

[21]McIntosh, "Understanding Baby Boomers," class notes, 12.

[22]George Barna, The Frog in the Kettle: What Christians Need to Know about Life in the Year 2000 (Ventura, CA: Regal Books, Gospel Light, 1990), 23.

[23]McIntosh, "Understanding Baby Boomers," class notes, 2.

[24]Sweet, "Seminary and Congregation," 107.

[25]"Talbot School of Theology Doctor of Ministry Program 1994 to 1996," Handbook, Talbot School of Theology, Biola University, La Mirada, CA, 3.

[26]George Barna, Today's Pastors: A Revealing Look at What Pastors Are Saying about Themselves, Their Peers and the Pressures They Face (Ventura, CA: Regal Books, Gospel Light, 1993), 34.

Chapter Four

What Do You Expect?

DAN RODRIGUEZ FELT LIKE THE ROPE in a tug-of-war. He had been the pastor of Heritage Church for four years and had discovered how conflicting expectations can stymie ministry. When he began ministry in the busy Northeastern college town his vision had been to help the church become more contemporary to maximize its impact among the college students.

He moved swiftly, making substantial changes in the style of the worship services. Organ and piano gave way to keyboards. Hymns gave way to choruses. The atmosphere became more casual. Dan persuaded church leaders to drop the church's evening service entirely in favor of an ambitious program of small groups. Dan was certain that the church would begin to attract the younger segment of the town's population. The actual results were disheartening.

Attendance began to drop off among long-time church members. Giving declined. Conflict developed. Dan was not naive. He knew there would be some conflict over his efforts. He was dismayed to discover that the conflict involved people he had believed were as committed as he was to reaching the college students. They were not upset by the new contemporary emphasis, but by the conflict itself. Dan began to realize he had underestimated the power of tradition. He had also underestimated the value that people placed on the existing network of relationships in the church. When his bold efforts began to threaten the fabric of that network, even those who believed in what he was doing were torn.

Dan's first response was to stay the course and ride out the storm. In time he began to realize that, with a significant segment of the church against him, his efforts were self-defeating. He eventually backed away from nearly everything he had advocated. The church returned to its traditional ways. Dan hoped that this would bring peace. It did not.

Those who had been upset at the changes remained upset and those who had wanted the changes were now also upset. There was a general lack of confidence in Dan's leadership. Attendance continued to slide. Power struggles worsened. Dan became disillusioned. He had wanted nothing more than to reach people for Christ. Now he had seriously damaged his church and effectively destroyed his own credibility.

Dan resigned under pressure. He had discovered that key people in any church have certain expectations of what a church and its pastor should be. Based in large part on tradition and personal preference, those expectations often set the agenda for ministry. They create invisible yet formidable walls beyond which a pastor moves only at his own risk. When Dan stepped outside those boundaries, his pastorate died a slow death.

Every pastor faces a set of congregational expectations. Some are biblical and reasonable. Many are neither. Biblical or not, those expectations and how a pastor deals with them can make or break his ministry. For a significant number of pastors, the subject of expectations is a sore one. Our survey found that unwritten congregational expectations along with resistance to leadership and change were the major factors in pastors' decisions to resign.[1]

Bob remembers a sermon he heard during a chapel service while in seminary. The speaker was a seasoned pastor. His sermon, "When Am I Going to Have a Normal Day?" focused on the daily realities of church life as compared to the idealistic notions he had cherished early in his ministry. He realized very early that what his people expected from him was very different from what he had always believed about pastoral ministry. He rewrote his own mental job description in order to conform to the expectations of his congregation and avoid congregational discord. Other pastors facing the same dilemma find themselves locked in conflict. Consider one such case.

To Dream the Impossible Dream: Meeting Unrealistic Expectations

Pastors dream of a church in which everyone is happy, no one complains, and there is 100% agreement that the pastor is doing a great job. Such churches do not exist. This is an impossible dream because people approach church with widely varying expectations of the ministry and its leadership. Even so, pastors regularly face pressure to keep as many people happy as possible. In order to effectively deal with this pressure, it is important to understand the nature and sources of congregational expectations.

External Expectations

Churchgoers have varying and often contradictory expectations of their pastor. This should not be surprising considering the variety of people and backgrounds represented in the average local church and the rapidly changing culture in which the church is struggling to define itself.

Today, any church containing more than one generation is a multi-cultural church. The differences between the pre-war generation and the celebrated baby boom generation create vastly different expectations when it comes to church. Members of "generation X," as those born after 1964 are now being called, have yet another set of expectations.

The older generation sees church in a traditional way. To this generation, the pastoral role should center on preaching and personal contact.[2]

Boomers have high expectations of the pastor in other areas:

> Churches that have targeted the baby boomers provide quality programs and facilities. They are committed to excellence but do not require blind loyalty. They strive to communicate on a level comparable to that which the baby boomer experiences in the best of the secular world. The church nursery rivals the day-care center down the street for attractiveness and cleanliness. Sermons are compelling and credible for the college-educated parishioner who is both well-read and well-traveled. High standards are maintained, whether in the matter of biblical truth and/or in the quality of Christian fellowship.[3]

The excellence and relevance demanded by boomers place a different set of expectations on the pastor. In addition to preaching and doing personal work, he now must administer an ever expanding array of programs. The expectations of generation X are not yet well-defined.

This ecclesiastical generation gap affects all areas of church life. The generations have vastly different tastes in music, different ideas about commitment, and different approaches to the Bible.

In addition to intergenerational conflict, today's church environment serves up an ever increasing menu of domestic dysfunction and trauma. Churchgoers often call upon pastors to intervene and/or counsel in times of domestic crisis. These troubled people tend to focus so intently on their own pain they are not capable of understanding what their insistent demands for attention do to those who provide it.[4]

These diverse problems and perspectives combine to create impossible expectations of a pastor. One man cannot consistently please three of the most different generations in history. Neither can he act as an administrator, teacher, facilitator, builder, mentor, counselor and all-around expert on life. The inherent conflicts in these roles are obvious, as is the fact that no pastor has enough hours in the day to do everything.

The New Testament indicates that all Christians have spiritual gifts with which to minister in the church (Rom. 12:3-8). There is no indication that any Christian has all of the gifts.

In challenging pastors to higher levels of commitment, well-meaning colleagues often unwittingly reinforce unrealistic expectations. A nationally known leader said at a conference that the pastorate "flies on two wings: leadership and ministry." Within these two areas he placed everything from articulating the church's vision to arriving before everyone else to turn on the lights.[5]

Unrealistic expectations tend to build upon themselves creating a crushing load for the minister, a load of which many members of the church remain ignorant.

> There is a downward spiral in unrealistic expectations in a church which harms everyone.
>
> First, the people become passive and dependent. Believing the pastor's education is what qualified him to minister, they quite logically conclude from this erroneous premise that they are unable to minister. The responsibility for ministry, therefore, falls completely on the pastor.
>
> The second step is to see the pastor as a professional who "gets paid for ministering," so they reason, "why should we do his job?" They reason falsely that the responsibility for ministry falls totally on the pastor.
>
> A third destructive attitude springs from their passivity and dependence. Passive, dependent individuals often become demanding people who heap increasing loads of responsibility for ministry on the pastor.[6]

The expectations don't always stop with the man in the pulpit. Churches sometimes have expectations of the pastor's family too. The qualifications of elders contained in the pastoral epistles require that a pastor's family demonstrate that the pastor is doing an adequate job as a husband and father (1 Tim. 3:2,4; Titus 1:6). This understanding is crucial. There are those who act as if the church is hiring the pastor's whole family. This is a bogus notion and one that goes way beyond the meaning of these passages. Yet some persist.

> Members of the clergy family are surrounded by expectations of all kinds: Who has the right to do what to the parsonage? What should the social boundaries between the clergy family and the congregation look like? Which family type is the most ideal? and so on. Parishioners often expect members of their "royal family" to be models of virtue in both church and family life. But the matter is hardly one sided. Members of the pastor's family also have ideas about how to fulfill their roles as leaders in the congregation as well as how to live together as a family. Thus, in the ecology of the clergy family, the congregation and family members interact with each other, attempting to define appropriate expectations and roles.[7]

These expectations can contribute to bitterness in the pastoral family who not only see the church as a competitor vying for time and attention, but also pick up on the frustration of the parents over pastoral expectations.[8] Our survey indicated that unwritten expectations of the pastoral family, while not at the top of the list of ministerial frustrations, are nevertheless a factor in one out of ten resignations.[9]

Internal Expectations

In addition to the unrealistic expectations created in the church environment, there are frequently unrealistic expectations at work within the pastor himself. These result from several things. He may have a faulty understanding of the pastoral role as presented in Scripture (1 Pet. 5:1-3 et al.). He may also react to imagined expectations. A pastor can easily interpret random comments or complaints about church life as expressions of expectation.[10] Some are and some aren't. Or he may try to emulate his mentors and other pastoral role models. The problem with this is that if the average pastor wrote down the combined strengths of all his pastoral role models, the resulting list would put Paul, Solomon, and Moses all to shame.[11]

The spiritual danger is that internal expectations tend to promote a performance theology within the pastor's own mind. He must succeed at fulfilling as many of the expectations as possible in order to feel worthwhile as an individual. This may directly contradict the message of grace he preaches, but that doesn't change the feelings of guilt he experiences as a result of his own failures. Chap Clark describes this "performance treadmill:"

> I felt guilty about my failings and shortcomings before I met Jesus, but nothing like I experienced afterward. Guilt took on a whole new meaning for me. Not only did I have to worry about my own legitimate failures, shortcomings, and hurts done to others, I now had to be constantly concerned that I was displeasing my God.[12]

" ... displeasing my God." This may be a secret fear of many pastors who struggle to meet every demand whether real or imagined. They must perform or risk facing the possibility that they are not good pastors and hence not pleasing to God.

Pastors must accept the biblical truth that they preach. As much as anyone else, pastors are "accepted in the beloved" (Eph. 1:6 KJV). God's love is not based on performance. Perhaps pastors should accept this and begin to obey the words of Scripture by ministering primarily in the sphere of their gifts. "For by the grace given me I say to every one of you: Do not think of yourself more highly than you ought, but rather think of yourself with sober judgment, in accordance with the measure of faith God has given you" (Rom. 12:3).

When a person can't admit his own limitations, he takes on roles that others can and should play. He fails to equip others to do the work of the ministry, something that is central to a biblical description of his role (Eph. 4:11-13). More importantly, he fails to rely on God. The results are often damaging.

Crash and Burn: The Effect of Unrealistic Expectations

The first effect of unrealistic expectations is the difficulty in measuring success. With so many different and ill-defined concepts of the pastoral role, a pastor doesn't know for sure what he should be doing so he isn't sure when he has succeeded at it. Listen to the sarcastic words from one pastor's journal.

If I wanted to drive a manager up the wall, I would make him responsible for the success of an organization and give him no authority. I would provide him with unclear goals, not commonly agreed upon by the organization. I would ask him to provide a service of an ill-defined nature, apply a body of knowledge having few absolutes, and staff his organization with only volunteers. I would expect him to work ten to twelve hours per day and have his work evaluated by a committee of 300 to 500 amateurs. I would call him a minister and make him accountable to God.[13]

In his book, *13 Fatal Errors Managers Make and How You Can Avoid Them*, Steven Brown lists as number six, "Forget the importance of profit."[14] He describes profit as the one ball you can't afford to drop. In other words, in a corporate setting the bottom line is the bottom line. But what is the bottom line in a church? Which ball should the pastor make certain he doesn't drop? If this question goes unanswered, a pastor feels he dare not drop any of them lest he fail the church. Eventually he may drop all of them.

This ambiguity robs a pastor of a sense of accomplishment. He is never finished and has never fully succeeded. Since this is the case, many pastors function with a profound sense of personal inadequacy and continual fear of impending failure. As Kent Hughes observes, "Every year thousands leave the ministry convinced they are failures."[15]

It also robs a pastor of a sense of normalcy, plunging him repeatedly into "crisis mode" and slowly turning him into a kind of ecclesiastical machine whose existence revolves around taking care of things at church. If it were not for that all–encompassing responsibility, many pastoral couples would not know how to define themselves.

Consider the feelings of a pastor's wife after her husband was fired from his pastorate. "It felt as though our lives had been vandalized. It was like someone had crept into our lives, stealing our most precious possessions and damaging our values."[16] Most are not fired, but many pastors feel like quitting because there is no joy in a life given totally and intensively to ill-defined success and shifting expectations.

Without any sense of regular accomplishment or normalcy, it is difficult to find rest. Stephen R. Covey suggests that one of the "seven habits of highly effective people" involves "sharpening the saw." He is referring to meaningful recreation as an essential element in the lives of effective people. He claims that this is essential to excellence in every area of life.[17] Covey didn't originate this idea. The concept of meaningful periodic rest is as old as Genesis. This kind of renewal comes too seldom for a pastor burning the candle at both ends to meet as many expectations as possible.

The ultimate result of unrealistic expectations is burnout and, for many, a departure from ministry. *Leadership's* survey of pastors found that 94% felt pressure to have an ideal family and 77% reported that their spouse felt pressure to be an ideal role model for a Christian family. No less than 63% said that congregational expectations create problems in their marriage.[18] An earlier survey indicated that 50% of pastors felt unable to meet the demands of the job.[19] In still another study, researchers found "that unrealistic expectations are a major factor in pastoral burnout."[20] Our survey results revealed that 47% cited unwritten congregational expectations as a factor in their decision to resign from their church.[21]

Donald P. Smith explains several of the internal conflicts that result from unclear and unrealistic expectations.

1. The crisis of *Integrity:* the feeling of falseness from a discrepancy between one's beliefs and one's true situation, and one's outer profession or activity.

2. The crisis of *Power:* a feeling that one lacks the authority, recognition, or power to influence a situation, partly at least because of feelings that the church itself is ineffectual.

3. The crisis of *Capacity:* a feeling that one lacks the ability to use the authority or power at his disposal.

4. The crisis of *Failure, or fear of Failure.*

5. The crisis of *Destination:* a concern for where the church is going in view of institutional ambiguity.

6. The crisis of *Role:* a concern for how one gets to the destination (including role conflict).

7. The crisis of *Meaning:* a concern for "What does it all add up to?"[22]

It all adds up to one thing: burnout. There is clearly a need for someone to define what a pastor is and what he is to do. There is a need to protect him from those well-meaning believers (including himself), who would continually expand the role.

The Biblical Way

The Bible addresses the issue of a pastor's role. Its guidelines make pastoral expectations manageable. There are three relevant biblical principles.

Equipping the Saints

The main role of a pastor is to equip the people of his church to carry out the work of the ministry (Eph. 4:11-12). It is not his job to accomplish the work of the ministry by himself. Great leaders from Moses to the apostles in Jerusalem have discovered the need to narrowly define their role and delegate to others tasks for which others are gifted (Exod. 18:13-26; Acts 6:2-4). This same responsibility is incumbent upon pastors.

Some expect pastors to perform all kinds of miscellaneous tasks based on false notions about shepherding. When Scripture uses the imagery of a shepherd to picture our Lord, the intent is to present a God who meets all of our needs (Ps. 23 et al.). Since pastors are "under-shepherds" (1 Pet. 5:4), it is tempting to apply the imagery of the Lord as a shepherd to the pastor. When this mind-set prevails, a pastor finds himself attempting the impossible task of meeting everyone's needs. He seeks to become a close friend and mentor to an ever increasing number of people. Only God can be that kind of shepherd. This is not the intent of Scripture for pastors. The term "pastor" meaning "shepherd" is the least common term for the office, appearing in noun or verb form in only a few contexts. Where it does appear, it refers specifically to just a few important tasks.

The Apostle Paul urged the overseers who were with him to "be shepherds over the church of God which he bought with his own blood" (Acts 20:28). In the following verses, Paul described false teachers as "savage wolves" who would prey on the flock. He urged the shepherds to guard against these wolves, reminding them of his own constant warnings (Acts 20:31). In this context, shepherding means guarding a church by warning people against false teaching.

I Peter 5:1-5 describes the work of shepherding as overseeing the flock. The Apostle Peter urged elders to undertake this task of leadership by being an example. There is no indication that leadership by example in this context means doing all kinds of miscellaneous tasks. Such would also contradict the model of delegation seen in the choosing of the first deacons in Acts 6. No, a pastor's example is to be that of a spiritually mature individual who is not greedy, but willing to serve in his capacity as an overseer (1 Pet. 5:2-3). In this context, shepherding is about being a leader. Taken together, these passages define the word "shepherd" as it applies to pastors. Shepherding involves teaching the truth, warning against falsehood, and leading by spiritual example. It does not involve any and every task that can be generally grouped under the heading "pastoral care."

The biblical pastor recognizes that his central task is preaching the whole counsel of God and leading by spiritual example. He offers vision, training, and oversight to a church that then carries out the work of the ministry. His is not the task of the church, but the task of leading the church. He cannot do it all. In accomplishing the work of the church, his role is to equip and delegate.

Using His Gifts

Second, the pastor is to minister in the sphere of his own gifts. Even though certain gifts are necessary for those God calls into the pastorate (he should have teaching and administration gifts), the presence of these gifts does not make pastors identical. There are no two pastors with exactly the same combination of abilities. One preaches well and struggles with administration. Another is a great administrator but is weak in preaching. Even among those with the same basic gifts, no two will do the same tasks in the same way or with the same results. The fact that different men have different abilities and therefore different ministries is evident in Scripture.

When the Corinthian church began to compare apostles, Paul pointed out the divine plan for different kinds of leaders: "I planted the seed, Apollos watered it, but God made it grow" (1 Cor. 3:6). No two apostles were alike. If they had been, the Corinthian church wouldn't have been choosing favorites. What was true in the days of the apostles is true today. It is therefore necessary for a pastor to do what he can do well with all of his strength and give the rest away. A pastor is to minister in the sphere of his gifts.

Working with Others

Third, the pastor is to work with other pastors who have different gifts. The three words for pastor in the New Testament all occur in plural form in single church contexts. "Paul and Barnabas appointed elders for them in each church" (Acts 14:23). Paul addressed the letter to the Philippians to "all the saints in Christ Jesus at Philippi, together with the overseers and deacons." In Acts 20, Paul addressed the "elders" at Ephesus, referring to them in verse 28 as "overseers" and "shepherds" (pastors). The biblical model of leadership in a local church is plural. This model of multiple leadership helps insure that a church will get a more balanced combination of gifted leaders than it could get with a "solo" pastor. It also relieves the individual shepherd of some of the pressure of expectations that go beyond his gifts. Scripture does not require that plural pastoral leadership involve additional paid pastoral staff. While full-time pastors deserve financial support (1 Cor. 9:7-11), there is no indication that all elders were full-time pastors. Lay elders can and should have an important leadership role in local churches. A pastor needs to work with other shepherds of different gifts.

*There are few areas more important to a pastor's continued success than the area of expectations. Your pastor **cannot and should not** meet every expectation voiced in your church. Instead, he must be a leader who reshapes them. The man who succeeds in ministry must define his role in a way that is biblical, that fits him, and that allows him to focus on the task at hand rather than on satisfying all those around him. Over time a pastor can shape the expectations of those around him. If he fails to do so, those expectations will shape him.*

You Can Help!

The task of reshaping expectations is a difficult one because the expectations come from so many sources. The only common denominator is the pastor himself. He is at the center of the varied expectations. It is therefore up to him to reshape them. You can help him by understanding the problem and encouraging him to deal with it. Here are five ways that you can help the pastor set up a job description everyone can live with.

1. Ask your pastor to define himself.

He should define both the biblical parameters of the job and the parameters of his own pastoral gifts. If he doesn't, others will. We sometimes identify with the pastor whose wife remarked, "God loves you and everyone else has a wonderful plan for your life." With all of the voices out there calling on the pastor to be this and do that, the only one who really knows what he can do is the pastor himself. John Bradley and Jay Carty emphasize the need for individuals to identify their own talents if they are to achieve excellence.

> Are you questioning how realistic it is to expect excellence in your life journey? Perhaps you're trying to walk down someone else's path. If so, you'll probably find it rough going. When you concentrate on the talents God has put within you, you'll start charting your personal path to excellence.[23]

By "define himself" we mean that, beyond having a biblical theology of the pastorate, the pastor should identify his own strengths and weaknesses. Many spiritual gift inventories are available as well as a plethora of leadership assessment instruments. The IDAK Group[24] provides an excellent series of tests and counseling designed to help an individual understand his unique combination of gifts, tendencies and values.

Even a simple process of feedback from responsible and discerning church members can be of great help. The pastor's own desires and natural tendencies can be revealing. Ask him, "What is your passion in ministry?" The answer may surprise you. The means may vary, but it is essential that the pastor and leaders of the church understand just who the man in the pulpit is and, more importantly, is not. Once you have identified your pastor's top strengths and weaknesses, you can assist him in writing a specific job description that reflects biblical priorities and details how he will lead in meeting those priorities. Without significant support from the leadership board and key people of the church this process will not move forward in any meaningful way.

2. Ask your pastor to communicate himself.

If the role of the pastor is to cast vision for the whole church,[25] surely it is up to him to communicate his own role in fulfilling that vision. This communication involves talking about his passions in ministry and frankly admitting that he has strengths in some areas but not in others. Carl Markum, a solo pastor in a small rural church, found that such admissions bring freedom from unrealistic expectations. His predecessor had strengths in the area of scholarship. He loved to study. His sermons were well-crafted and well-received. Everyone in the church knew of this strength. It was obvious and appreciated. On the other hand, this pastor had a weakness when it came to some of the personal work. He did his best, but had a tendency to avoid that area in favor of his first love—books. He never really dealt openly with the subject of his own inherent strengths and weaknesses. Consequently, some churchgoers blamed him as if he had deliberately neglected their needs.

Carl's experience with the same group has been different. He told them up front that he is not strong in the area of counseling. As a result there is less tension over his weaknesses in that area. People don't automatically think him uncaring. Most understand that he simply lacks the inherent talents for a strong counseling ministry. Of course there are still those who believe that every pastor should be a good counselor. These folks want a "renaissance" pastor who can do everything well. Fortunately such people are few. Carl has greater freedom from unrealistic expectations than did his predecessor because he openly admits his weaknesses. If a pastor is open about his own expectations of himself based on his God-given strengths and weaknesses, most people will eventually adopt similar expectations.

3. Ask your pastor to commit himself to doing a few things well.

Pastor Gary Harrison suggests that small churches focus on one or two strengths, working to improve them until the church gains real expertise in those areas.[26] This approach works well because a small church only has the resources to pursue a few things with excellence. The same can be said of a pastor. He has a limited number of talents.

If he acts the part of the generalist—a jack of all trades—he practically guarantees mediocrity. If, on the other hand, he focuses on his strengths, working to improve them over time, he will find the path to excellence in his ministry. Help your pastor find this path.

4. Ask your pastor to delegate himself.

If he focuses on only a few areas and devotes larger segments of time to them, delegation isn't just desirable, it's essential. Vernon Grounds, chancellor and president emeritus of Denver Seminary, says that if God gave him a second chance to be a pastor he would do several things differently. Among other changes, he would make more efficient use of time so as to live out his real priorities.[27] Delegation of tasks is perhaps the single greatest aid to efficiency any leader has. Not only does it allow the leader to focus on his "real priorities," it is good for the church, allowing the body to minister to one another as God intended.

This may be difficult since many pastors, while overworked, find it difficult to give work away. Take the work from your pastor and hold him accountable for doing only those things within the sphere of an agreed-upon job description.

5. Finally, protect your pastor from pastor abusers.

"Ministers spend needless time and energy on Christian believers who are unlovable and do not want to change."[28] In every church there is the proverbial squeaky wheel who acts as if he has a right to as much pastoral "grease" as he can get. Given free rein, such people absorb the greater part of a pastor's energy and shut down his ability to think strategically. Unfortunately, many churches expect their pastor to focus on just such people. Success is measured by whether or not the pastor can keep people happy. Your pastor will never be able to define himself and his ministry if he is continually focusing on the intractable problems of a few high-maintenance individuals. Pastor Matt Hannan suggests strongly that pastors need to set limits in order to be effective: "If I am spending all of my time thinking about a person, that person needs to go away."[29] In a recent visit to an effective, growing church the pastor was asked about his obvious success in ministry. He attributed the success of his ministry to three things: the church's prayer life, their team leadership, and the office secretaries who zealously guard the pastors against needless intrusion by the church's chronic squeaky wheels.

–End Chapter Four–

[1]Pastoral Survey, see appendix.

[2]Charles U. Wagner, The Pastor: His Life and Work (Schaumburg, IL: Regular Baptist Press, 1976), 23-24.

[3]Leith Anderson, Dying for Change (Minneapolis: Bethany House Publishers, 1990), 85.

[4]H. B. London and Neil B. Wiseman, Pastors at Risk: Help for Pastors, Hope for the Church (Wheaton, IL: Victor Books, Scripture Press Publications, 1993), 58-59.

[5]Elmer Towns: sermon preached at NWCBA Annual Conference in Tacoma, WA, on 9 March 1995.

[6]London and Wiseman, Pastors at Risk, 56.

[7]Cameron Lee and Jack Balswick, Life in a Glass House: The Minister's Family in Its Unique Social Context, Ministry Resources Library series (Grand Rapids, MI: Zondervan Publishing House, 1989), 113.

[8]Michael E. Phillips, "Fatal Reaction: Antidotes to PK Poisoning," Leadership Journal 13, no. 4 (Fall 1992): 28.

[9]Pastoral Survey, see appendix.

[10]London and Wiseman, Pastors at Risk, 58.

[11]Richard P. Hansen, "The Sound of Clashing Expectations," Leadership Journal 5, no. 3 (Summer 1984): 79-80.

[12]Chap Clark, The Performance Illusion (Colorado Springs, CO: NavPress, 1993), 16-17.

[13]James Hamilton, The Pair in Your Parsonage (Kansas City: Beacon Hill, 1982), 10, citing an anonymous minister's journal; quoted in London and Wiseman, Pastors at Risk, 54.

[14]W. Steven Brown, 13 Fatal Errors Managers Make and How You Can Avoid Them (New York: Berkley Books, 1985), 79.

[15]Kent and Barbara Hughes, Liberating Ministry from the Success Syndrome (Wheaton, IL: Tyndale House Publishers, 1988), 10.

[16]Gary D. Preston, "Terminated: Finding Your Identity When You've Lost Your Job," Leadership Journal 13, no. 4 (Fall 1992): 60; citing his wife.

[17]Stephen R. Covey, The Seven Habits of Highly Effective People: Restoring the Character Ethic (New York: Simon & Schuster, 1989), 287.

[18]David Goetz, "Is the Pastor's Family Safe at Home?" Leadership Journal 13, no. 4 (Fall 1992): 39-41.

[19]Richard A. Blackmon, "Survey of Pastors," in "The Hazards of the Ministry," Psy.D. diss., Graduate School of Psychology, Fuller Theological Seminary, Pasadena, CA, 1984.

[20]Malony and Hunt, "The Psychology of Clergy," citing William Moore; quoted in London and Wiseman, Pastors at Risk, 58.

[21]Pastoral Survey, see appendix.

[22]Donald P. Smith, Clergy in the Cross Fire: Coping with Role Conflicts in the Ministry (Philadelphia: Westminster Press, 1973), 65-66.

[23]John Bradley and Jay Carty with Russ Korth, Unlocking Your Sixth Suitcase: How to Love What You Do and Do What You Love (Colorado Springs, CO: NavPress, Navigators, 1991), 18.

[24]The IDAK Group, 7931 N.E. Halsey, Portland, OR 97213.

[25]Rick Warren, Defined Purposes: How to Lay a Foundation for Growth, Audio tape of message by Rick Warren, presented at the 1990 Saddleback Church Growth Conference (Mission Viejo, CA: The Encouraging Word).

[26]Gary Harrison, "The Making of a Good Little Church," Leadership Journal 7, no. 3 (Summer 1986): 93.

[27]Vernon Grounds, lecture presented in "DM 824, The Pastor's Spiritual and Emotional Health," 12-16 July 1993, Talbot School of Theology, Biola University, La Mirada, CA, class notes by author.

[28]Lucille Lavender, They Cry, Too! What You Always Wanted to Know about Your Minister but Didn't Know Whom to Ask (New York: Hawthorn Books, W. Clement Stone, 1976), 52.

[29]Matt Hannan, "Retooling Traditional Churches," lecture presented in "Min 801, Pastor's Symposium, Contemporary Models of ministry: Reaching Baby Boomers," 15-19 October 1990, Talbot School of Theology, Biola University, La Mirada, CA, class notes.

Chapter Five

The Invisible Man

CHURCHES EXPECT MUCH FROM THEIR PASTORS. Ironically, in many important areas, the pastor often goes without meaningful accountability. While accountability is a fashionable word today in ministry, it certainly is not a new concept. The Bible has much to say on the subject. Too often in today's world, we have seen pastoral disasters that could have been prevented by proper accountability. Consider one such catastrophe:

Harry Mastersen did not know what to say. The voice on the phone sounded distinctly uncomfortable. "Pastor Mike has resigned!" Harry had called to ask advice of his friend, an experienced and successful urban pastor. Pastor Mike's church had grown steadily during his tenure as few churches do. The growth resulted largely from his own consummate pastoral skill. As a result, other pastors sought out his advice. He seemed happy to help. But not on this day.

The news of Mike's sudden resignation made Harry forget all about his own problems. He had a sinking feeling. What was it the voice *wasn't* saying? Harry didn't know how to ask. "Really? Well w-w-where did he go?" He stammered.

"He, umm, hasn't gone anywhere. He is ... under church discipline for marital infidelity." Harry didn't work for the rest of the day.

The story came out slowly. Rumors abounded. For a time, Pastor Mike rebelled against the discipline of his church. He seemed on the verge of walking away from his family and faith. Then he repented. In time he came to a denominational meeting to ask forgiveness of his colleagues. It was there that the underlying causes of his failure began to emerge. Mike and his wife, Verna, were married as much to their ministry as to each other. They paid a price for their success in relational currency. Their marriage slowly crumbled as their self-imposed job description demanded more than they could safely give. Others saw the signs but there was no one to hold Mike or Verna accountable. No one checked on Mike's spiritual well-being. No one asked, "How many hours are you working anyway?" Only after the marital meltdown occurred did the church board realize that Mike had been doing the work of at least two staff people for years. Sadly, the same lack of accountability that allowed Mike to burn himself out in the name of ministry also allowed him in his spiritual exhaustion to carry on an affair with a female staff member under the noses of the church leadership. Verna made the discovery that led to Mike's resignation.

Mike still grieves the loss of his ministry. He loved being a pastor. He was born for it. There are many who would urge him to get back in, but he believes that he has lost credibility and cannot biblically return. He also grieves the loss of his marriage. Today, Verna has a new last name. The tragedy is that their painful divorce could have been prevented. It wouldn't even have been difficult.

The Reality Check

Occasionally we hear journalists refer to a "reality check." Usually the phrase refers to checking the facts before accepting the assertions of various political figures. The reality check is a real and regular part of all of our lives. All of us have to regularly correct our own perceptions with objective facts in order to function in the real world. The Bible encourages people to seek such corrections. "Whoever loves discipline loves knowledge, but he who hates correction is stupid" (Prov. 12:1) "Wounds from a friend can be trusted, but an enemy multiplies kisses" (Prov. 27:6). The New Testament urges believers to hold one another accountable for their actions. "Brothers, if someone is caught in a sin, you who are spiritual should restore him gently" (Gal. 6:1).

Objective input that corrects us from time to time is not just important spiritually, but psychologically as well. The *Taylor-Johnson Temperament Analysis*, a well-validated and respected personality inventory, measures, among other traits, a person's subjectivity. The authors define "subjective" as, "emotional, self-absorbed and illogical." By contrast, "'objective' is defined as "fair-minded, reasonable, and logical." It is the "self-absorbed" quality that really differentiates a subjective person from an objective one. A highly subjective person tends to be biased in his or her perceptions because his or her only standard of measurement is self. Such a person cannot make objective, nondefensive comparisons with the perceptions of others. He or she is often impaired relationally and vocationally as a result. An objective person, on the other hand, is able to see things as they are. He or she is able to be "fair-minded" and "reasonable." [1] Such a person allows reality to correct his or her perceptions.

Scripture urges that leaders be held accountable for their performance as well as their morality. "The elders who direct the affairs of the church well are worthy of double honor, especially those whose work is preaching and teaching" (1 Tim. 5:17). Scripture requires an active, ongoing evaluation of a pastor's performance. This is accountability. Len Kageler, a youth pastor in Seattle, Wash., was reluctant to initiate a system of performance appraisal for himself and the rest of the staff. One reason: no one likes to face criticism. Then he realized that most of the people on the church board regularly faced and profited by such evaluations in their employment. He went ahead and initiated a performance appraisal system and has never been sorry he did. [2]

Pastors not only need an objective evaluation of their performance, but they need an objective evaluation of our manner of life, their integrity. A few verses after commanding that elders who do excellent work be accorded double honor, Paul addressed this other facet of pastoral accountability: "Those who sin are to be rebuked publicly so that the others may take warning" (1 Tim. 5:20). Here, the accountability is clearly in the area of morality. In neither area is accountability presented as optional. Patrick Morley writes,

> One of the greatest reasons men get into trouble is that they don't have to answer to anyone for their lives. Ask around. You will learn that very few men have built accountability into their Christian lifestyle. It is the *missing link* of Christianity.
>
> Some of us have invested our whole life to "be our own boss" for the very goal that we *won't* have to answer to anyone! Others of us, confidential by nature, don't want someone else intruding into our private lives. And still others of us have an interest, but we are unsure of what accountability actually is, and how to go about it.
>
> Every day men fail morally, spiritually, relationally, and financially; not because they don't want to succeed, but because they have *blind spots* and *weak spots* which they surmise they can handle on their own. They can't. And they lose their families, their businesses, their jobs, their savings, and damage their relationship with God because no one is there to ask, "How? Why? What? and Who?" —the hard questions.

Some men have spectacular failures where in a moment of passion they abruptly burst into flames, crash, and burn. But the more common way men get into trouble evolves from hundreds of tiny decisions—decisions which go undetected—that slowly, like water tapping on a rock, wear down a man's character. Not blatantly or precipitously, but subtly, over time, we get caught in a web of cutting corners and compromise, self-deceit and wrong thinking, which goes unchallenged by anyone in our lives.[3]

Without an objective voice reminding us of reality, pastors can fool themselves by overlooking serious flaws in their attitudes and/or behaviors until willful blindness causes disaster. Whether it is a simple matter of job performance or the more complex and serious matter of integrity, pastors, like everyone else, cannot go it alone. They need others to bring us the reality check.

The No-Account Vocation

It's not that pastors lack input. There is no shortage of people sharing their opinions. What pastors lack is *meaningful* input. Pastors often go without objective evaluation of their performance or their integrity. Our survey of pastors who have recently resigned asked whether those pastors had been regularly held accountable in any or all of eleven areas. These included use of time, daily quiet time, prayer life, rest, exercise, entertainment habits, thought life, family relationships, marriage, handling of money, and continuing education. Only 27% of pastors reported being held accountable in the area of time usage. Most pastors reported no accountability relationship whatsoever. Significantly, 23% said that lack of accountability played a part in their decision to resign.[4] The stories behind those statistics are often similar to that of Mike and Verna.

One reason for this lack of objective evaluation and accountability is in the nature of pastoral work. A pastor works largely alone. The old saw about a pastor being the man who is invisible six days per week and indecipherable on the seventh is at least half-true. Most parishioners have no idea how he spends his time. Nor do many leaders in the church. He is the invisible man. Even in situations where there is a multiple pastoral staff, the individual staffers often work alone. It's just the nature of much of pastoral work.

The nature of the man often adds to the isolation. Sinful human beings naturally resist accountability. Our Lord said that when He came into the world He represented moral and spiritual light. However, mankind rejected that light preferring their own darkened moral and spiritual state. "This is the verdict: Light has come into the world, but men loved darkness instead of light because their deeds were evil" (John 3:19). Old habits die hard. Even among Christians, independence from accountability has always been a serious temptation. The writer to the Hebrews urged his readers to "spur one another on toward love and good deeds." He advocated nothing less than accountability for growth in Christ. Sadly, immediately following this admonition, he pleads, "and let us not give up meeting together, *as some are in the habit of doing*" (Heb. 10:24-25). Even in those early days, there were believers who kept themselves apart from others. They avoided, among other things, the accountability on spiritual issues afforded by regular interaction with other believers. This is an especially subtle trap for pastors since they are regarded as "a cut above" in matters of spirituality. It is difficult for a person who is supposed to have all of the answers to admit to an area of struggle or temptation. Pride comes even more strongly into play. Louis McBurney suggests that many pastors have a dread of dependency that allows them to be "gracious helper[s]" but "unrealistically uncomfortable in the position of need."[5] Four problems arise, however, from resistance to accountability.

The Ivory-Tower Syndrome

Ministers are sometimes accused of having an "impractical often escapist attitude marked by aloof lack of concern with or interest in practical matters or urgent problems."[6] In other words, they are thought to be in an ivory tower. While this is certainly not a true assessment of most ministers, most are sometimes isolated from their people. When a pastor isolates himself or neglects to ask for meaningful feedback from his church members, he passes up the opportunity to learn from them. He effectively retreats to an ivory tower.

Solomon's son, Rehoboam, made the biggest mistake of his young life when he failed to heed the advice of wise older men in his court. They urged him to listen to the people and lessen their tax burden. Instead, he listened to his cronies who urged him to ignore the people and raise taxes. His decision in favor of the latter brought about a civil war from which the kingdom never recovered (2 Chr. 12f.). He was out of touch with the reality of his people's suffering. His was an ivory-tower decision. Such decisions can be equally disastrous in the life of a pastor and church. The ivory tower is avoided when there is strong accountability.

Poor Performance

When excellence prevails, God is pleased. The New Testament urges Christians to maintain excellent standards in their work. "Whatever you do, work at it with all your heart, as working for the Lord, not for men" (Col. 3:23). The same standards apply to pastors: "If anyone speaks, he should do it as one speaking the very words of God" (1 Pet. 4:11). Objective evaluation increases performance in business, in sports, in school and, yes, in ministry. In his book, *Managing for the Future*, renowned management expert Peter F. Drucker argues that in order to be competitive in the twenty-first century, one of the urgent needs of business in the United States is for management accountability.[7] What is true in business is also true in the pastorate.

Ted Engstrom believes that all Christian leaders need to commit themselves to excellence through accountability. "Excellence is a *measurement*, and that assumes a standard of *accountability*."[8] A textbook on pastoral ministry illustrates this need:

> The easiest place in the world to be lazy is in the ministry. The reason for this is obvious. The pastor is his own boss. He can be easy on himself and still give the impression of being very busy about the Lord's work.[9]

We once heard of a pastor who felt that he had to get his Sunday morning sermon out of the way before he began studying for the evening sermon. He therefore put his Sunday evening sermons together in a few short hours on Sunday afternoons. In no job where accountability is practiced would an individual be allowed to continue performing in such a mediocre fashion. Yet people would meet him at the door and say, "Good sermon, pastor." What else could they comfortably say? If a pastor has no objective means of evaluating his performance, he is more likely to "be easy on himself." His chances of reaching excellence while maintaining a balanced life are diminished. His ability to grow from his mistakes is diminished. His level of satisfaction with his life and work are diminished too. The resulting mediocrity effects more than himself. If the leader is allowed to be less than he can be, the church will also suffer from his poor performance.

Self-Pity

In the absence of the accountability afforded by continual contact with others, one human tendency is to exaggerate our woes and underestimate our blessings. The Israelites certainly did this while they wandered in the desert. They were forever denouncing Moses for leading them out of Egypt, a land "flowing with milk and honey" (Num. 16:13) and into the desert to die. Talk about a distorted perspective! In reality, God was leading them out of *slavery* in Egypt *toward* a land flowing with milk and honey. The same kind of distortion can occur in the mind of a pastor wandering in the desert of isolation. Spurgeon wrote of this tendency, referring to its symptoms as "The Minister's Fainting Fits."[10] Pastors still have them. Louis McBurney tells a story of a man facing loss of perspective as a result of isolation.

> Recently I was having lunch with an Episcopalian priest. A warm, outgoing man of middle age, he shared with me an experience of a few years before. He had become disillusioned with his ministry, questioned his calling and commitment, and was at the end of his rope. The most agonizing aspect of his dilemma was having no one with whom he felt he could share his hurt. He felt threatened at the prospect of confiding in a parishioner, he feared that his bishop would blackball him, and he was embarrassed to confess to a colleague. In despair, he simply disappeared to a large city and lost himself for a few days. There, in physical loneliness, he found the peace unavailable in his emotional isolation within the crowd at home.[11]

This man was certain of things that probably weren't true. Most likely, there was *someone* in whom he could confide. Simply dropping out for a few days was not the best approach, especially considering the temptations a big city presents to a man alone and in a state of spiritual uncertainty. Isolation results in subjectivity, and subjectivity results in self-pitying conclusions and poor decisions. As in this case, the self-pitying perspective that sometimes accompanies isolation breeds further isolation and greater self-pity. It becomes a vicious circle. Many good people have fallen into this trap.

Elijah found himself in such a state. Having won an enormous spiritual victory over the prophets of Baal, he nevertheless became frightened of Jezebel's threats against his life. He fled into isolation. After just one day, he collapsed in exhaustion and begged God to take his life. His perspective had become distorted. After fleeing still further, God asked Elijah to explain why he was there. His answer: "I am the only one left, and now they are trying to kill me too" (1 Kings 19:14). God reassured him that there were yet 7,000 others (1 Kings 19:18). Elijah returned to circulation and became effective once again.

Regular accountability can prevent the kind of self-pity that starts this self-defeating cycle. Elijah needed someone to come alongside him and remind him that a God who could bring down fire from heaven to consume his offering could certainly protect him from the queen. He needed to be humbled by the truth that this was God's battle and not his alone. He needed to know that there were others out there and that they needed him. He had no right to flee. Many pastors need the same reality check, especially on Monday.

Temptation

Perhaps the most dangerous result of pastoral isolation is that the absence of accountability provides fertile soil for all kinds of temptations. King David provides the most egregious example: During a time when he was idle and alone with his most trusted leaders, David committed adultery with Bathsheba (2 Sam. 11). The consequences were enormous. Bathsheba became pregnant. David had Uriah, her husband, killed and then took her as his wife in order to cover his sin. The child born from that union died and David's family experienced judgment for years to come. Interestingly enough, he didn't repent until Nathan the prophet confronted him. Nathan held him accountable. If he had experienced a higher level of accountability for his actions and thoughts earlier on, he might never have committed the sin in the first place.

Human nature hasn't changed. Tom Eisenman, equipping minister at Community Presbyterian Church in Danville, Calif., lists six major temptations which men face today. These include: "the temptation to be macho, the temptation of sexual lust, the temptation to have an affair, the temptation to wield power, the temptation to love money, and the temptation to be perfect."[12] Other lists may vary, but one conclusion that cannot be denied is that any temptation is more powerful in an atmosphere of low accountability. Eisenman goes on to list steps toward deliverance from temptations. A major part of this deliverance is "access[ing] accountable relationships."[13]

There was a time when society was less mobile, communities more tight-knit, and pastoral tenures considerably longer. This combination of circumstances provided for greater accountability than tends to exist today in our disconnected, highly mobile culture. But this is the world in which we live. In order to prevent possible disastrous consequences, we must take steps to provide for the accountability that seems to be lacking today.

The Accountable Pastor

While "accountability" has become a buzz word, it really is an old concept. Paul regularly submitted himself to the accountability of those to whom he preached:

> You are witnesses, and so is God, of how holy, righteous and blameless we were among you who believed. For you know that we dealt with each of you as a father deals with his own children, encouraging, comforting and urging you to live lives worthy of God, who calls you into his kingdom and glory (1 Thess. 2:10-12).

He also urged the churches to hold pastors accountable to high spiritual standards (1 Tim. 3:1-7; 5:19-25; Titus 1:6-9). A careful reading of these passages reveals that pastors are to be held accountable for their performance as well as for their moral and ethical conduct. Accountability is an intensely biblical concept.

It also happens to be effective. Management author Peter Drucker is sold on accountability for managers. Why? Because it works, that's why. Bobb Beihl agrees: "Evaluation precedes growth and improvement."[14] Another author writes succinctly, "Success and accountability [are] linked."[15] Perhaps Eugene Peterson says it best when he applies the concept to pastors:

> There is a saying among physicians that the doctor who is his own doctor has a fool for a doctor. It means, as I understand it, that the care of the body is a complex business and requires cool, detached judgment. We not only have bodies, we *are* bodies, and so none of us is capable of untainted objectivity regarding our own bodies. All of us, physicians included, want coddling, not healing. We prefer comfort to wholeness. And we can deceive ourselves about ourselves endlessly.[16]

Accountability is simply essential. It carries the endorsement of Scripture as well as that of countless believing and unbelieving authors dealing with the subject of leadership. It is particularly relevant to our discussion of pastors and why they quit. We believe that simple obedience to Scripture in this one area would make an immeasurable difference. Not only would accountability help pastors during the times of crisis that often lead directly to their professional demise, but also, properly implemented, it would address many of the underlying causes of such crises thus preventing them from ever developing. This is the real value of accountability.

> Remember, Dostoesvsky was correct when he wrote that human beings prefer miracle, mystery and authority to freedom and faith. That makes it a great temptation for ministers to substitute themselves, aided by their charisma, for the Divine. Accountability to other brothers and sisters in the body of Christ helps bring that temptation under control.[17]

Don't assume that because your pastor is a spiritual leader, he is therefore exempt from human frailty. He is not. Don't leave him to walk alone in his spiritual journey. Keep him grounded in reality. Encourage him, but hold him accountable to biblical standards and to some sensible guidelines that will minimize his isolation and temptations. Don't allow him to become a casualty of the ministry. The strongest statement we can make is this: If you come alongside your pastor and help him with affirmation and accountability, you will probably never know how much good you did or how much harm you helped prevent.

You Can Help!

Accountability by its very nature requires a commitment from more than one person. Often it is the person to whom accountability is due who must take the initiative. We believe it is the spiritual responsibility of the church to hold its pastor accountable in a number of ways. This is highly important if you wish to help your pastor survive and thrive in ministry. You can help.

1. Ask your pastor to work with people rather than alone whenever possible.

This involves taking others with him when he visits or travels. It may also mean involving others in counseling. It will certainly involve delegating tasks to others and then working with them as they serve. This will accomplish several objectives. First, your pastor will be able to be a more effective disciple-maker. "And the things you have heard me say in the presence of many witnesses entrust to reliable men who will also be qualified to teach others" (2 Tim. 2:2). Discipleship doesn't happen by your pastor working alone. Second, others will be encouraged to use their gifts in ministry resulting in a healthier church. Third, your pastor will benefit by getting to know more people in the church on a deeper level. This can only enhance his ministry. Last but not least, your pastor will not be isolated. He will be spending more of his time in the real world working with real people. This provides a natural kind of accountability. According to W. Steven Brown, the *"13 Fatal Errors Managers Make"* include these four: "fail[ure] to develop people, try[ing] to control results instead of influencing thinking, failure to train people, and refus[ing] to accept personal accountability."[18] It is significant that Brown calls these "fatal errors." It is equally significant that all four are addressed by this one simple strategy.

2. Offer your pastor regular performance reviews.

Len Kageler suggests involving significant people from several groups in this process. These include "staff, secretaries, interns, and custodial staff, members of the governing board, and others in the church with whom [you] have close ministry contact."[19] Many denominations offer questionnaires for use in performance reviews. You may wish to customize a performance review for your own situation. We would suggest looking at several before writing your own.

3. Enter into a mutual accountability relationship with your pastor.

If you are a man, another way you can help is to offer to enter into a mutual accountability relationship with your pastor based on a previously arranged list of criteria. In this way you can hold each other accountable for specific areas of responsibility without threat. Warning: such lists are only as good as the commitment of the people involved to honesty and transparency. They are not a magic wand, but they are a useful tool if conscientiously applied.

4. A variation of the accountability relationship is an accountability group in which several men, including the pastor, take part.

Such a group should involve men who take their spiritual walk seriously and are up to the scrutiny. They should be trustworthy men who are capable of keeping a confidence and who do not hold an unrealistic view of pastors as sinners-emeritus. Ted W. Engstrom suggests that leaders need three kinds of people to whom they can be accountable: "a *Timothy*" to whom they can give themselves, "a *Barnabas*" to encourage them, and "a *peer group*."[20] A peer group consists of men with whom the pastor has a lot in common. Often peers are people of one's own profession, although this is not necessary. Many pastors find it difficult to maintain anything but a pastoral relationship with members of their church. If you don't have the kind of relationship to your pastor that would allow for an accountability group, you may want to suggest to him that he enter into such a relationship with other pastors. In fact, you may want to hold him accountable for it.

–End Chapter Five–

[1]Robert M. Taylor and Lucile P. Morrison, Taylor-Johnson Temperament Analysis Manual, 1984 rev. (Los Angeles: Psychological Publications, 1984), 9.

[2]Len Kageler, "Performance Reviews: Worth the Trouble?" Leadership Journal 6, no. 3 (Summer 1985): 26.

[3]Patrick M. Morley, The Man in the Mirror: Solving the 24 Problems Men Face (Brentwood, TN: Wolgemuth & Hyatt, 1989), 273.

[4]Pastoral Survey, see appendix.

[5]Louis McBurney, Every Pastor Needs a Pastor (Waco, TX: Word Books, 1977), 63.

[6]Merriam Webster's New Collegiate Dictionary, 10th ed., s.v. "ivory tower."

[7]Peter F. Drucker, Managing for the Future: The 1990s and Beyond (New York: Truman Talley Books/Dutton, 1992), 246-247.

[8]Ted Engstrom, High Performance: The Best of Ted Engstrom, comp. Robert C. Larson (San Bernadino, CA: Here's Life Publishers, 1988), 281.

[9]Charles U. Wagner, The Pastor: His Life and Work (Schaumburg, IL: Regular Baptist Press, 1976), 229.

[10]C. H. Spurgeon, Lectures to My Students (Grand Rapids: Zondervan Publishing House, 1980), 154.

[11]McBurney, Every Pastor Needs a Pastor, 61.

[12]Tom L. Eisenman, Temptations Men Face: Straightforward Talk on Power, Money, Affairs, Perfectionism, Insensitivity (Downers Grove, IL: InterVarsity Press, 1990), Table of Contents.

[13]Eisenman, Temptations Men Face, 202.

[14]Bobb Biehl and Ted W. Engstrom, Increasing Your Boardroom Confidence (Sisters, OR: Questar Publishing, 1988), 193.

[15]Hudson T. Armerding, The Heart of Godly Leadership (Wheaton, IL: Crossway Books, Good News Publishers, 1992), 168.

[16]Eugene H. Peterson, Working the Angles: The Shape of Pastoral Integrity (Grand Rapids, MI: William B. Eerdmans Publishing Co., 1987), 165.

[17]Vernon Grounds, "Appendix: Accountability Guidelines," in class notes for "Pastor's Spiritual and Emotional Health" (See appendix F of this document).

[18]W. Steven Brown, 13 Fatal Errors Managers Make and How You Can Avoid Them (New York: Berkley Books, 1985), Table of Contents.

[19]Kageler, "Performance Reviews: Worth the Trouble?", 27.

[20]Engstrom, High Performance, 280.

Chapter Six

Stampeding The Sacred Cows

AS A BOY, we used to watch "westerns" on television. Often the plot involved a cattle drive. Invariably, something would spook the cattle, touching off a stampede. When that happened, no one was safe. Blind fear caused those longhorns to trample everything in their path. It reminds us of what happens when someone changes things in a church. Every modern pastor knows the difficulty involved in changing church programs and priorities when the old ones have been in place long enough to be canonized. These priorities and programs are not called sacred cows for nothing. First, it is "sacrilege" to touch them and, second, when the pastor does, he often gets hoof prints all over him! Listen to the true stories of two pastors with different approaches to change.

In 1992, Bill Weathers became the pastor of Skyline Community Church. He inherited a church with a past. Barely four years old, Skyline had begun as the result of a church split and had never really prospered. In the two years before Pastor Bill's arrival, the decline had become serious and members talked of closing the doors. Bill accepted the church's call with the clear understanding that he would initiate changes in order to reverse the church's decline. During the eleven months of his tenure, the pace of change was nothing short of furious.

The name "Skyline" was not the original name of the church. The church adopted it shortly after Bill's ministry began. Along with the change in name, the church changed its constitution, adopting an entirely new purpose statement and form of church government. The church also changed its denominational affiliation. These decisions took place in a single business meeting (!) and were followed by still others. These included a shift to a contemporary style of worship and initiation of "flock" groups in lieu of the traditional prayer meeting. The church building was also remodeled from top to bottom.

While all of this was taking place, attendance grew steadily from 35 to an average of 185 due, in part, to a healthy emphasis on evangelism.

There was a new sense of excitement and hope.

Then it happened. Bill suddenly resigned. Less than a year into a highly successful ministry, in the midst of a whirlwind of change that had stunned the "church pillars," he left. He was exhausted. The change had not come without fierce resistance. This resistance along with the frenetic pace which Bill himself set had taken its toll. He left the ministry entirely.

Bewildered and hurt, the church entered into a period of controversy and power struggles during which some of the progress that had been made was lost. For Skyline and its pastor, change was costly.

Jack Nelson pastored an entirely different kind of church. Like Skyline, Second Memorial was very traditional. However, unlike Bill's church, Second Memorial didn't carry the baggage of controversy arising from Skyline's acrimonious beginning. It was a stable church. It was also a complacent one.

Jack worked for change, although at a much slower pace. This was not the result of a deliberate strategy, but of Jack's temperament combined with inexperience. In his five-year pastorate, the church made many of the same changes as Skyline. They dropped their prayer meeting in favor of small groups. They updated their services and greatly expanded the church's youth ministry. The church doubled in size over the five-year period.

While he changed much, Jack also left many things alone. The church's name remained the same as did its cumbersome system of government. The church didn't significantly upgrade its facilities. Jack identified with Leith Anderson's story about a pastor charged with bringing a church up to speed. In that story, the pastor confidently asserted that the church would soon enter the nineteenth century. "You mean the 'twentieth century!'" a church leader corrected. The pastor replied, "We're going to take this one century at a time!"[1]

In the end, Jack too resigned. He was tired of the uphill struggle to change the thinking of key people who saw no virtue in change. He too had had enough. The only difference was that it had taken Jack five years to reach a state of exhausted frustration because he had pushed more slowly. Also, because the changes had taken place more slowly, the church was not plunged into conflict as a result of his departure. Other than that, the results were similar. For the pastors involved, the results were identical.

Pastors have different ways of acting as change agents, but regardless, change is one of the most difficult facets of modern ministry. The persistent question: Why is change so difficult for churches and so painful for pastors?

The Need for Change

The need for change in the way we do church is not agreed upon by all. That's the problem. In many places, traditional methods employed for decades in American evangelical churches no longer work. Yet, there are many who refuse to see the need for change. Trying to force that change is a lot like pouring new wine into old wineskins.[2] Jesus asserted, "No one pours new wine into old wineskins. If he does, the wine will burst the skins, and both the wine and the wineskins will be ruined. No, he pours new wine into new wineskins" (Mark 2:22). Similarly, when new methods and forms of worship are introduced into a traditional body of believers, the resulting controversy is often damaging and more than a bit messy. Nevertheless, the change is necessary and ultimately inevitable for two very important reasons.

The Decline of the Traditional Church

Traditional ways of doing church are in trouble. The old neighborhood church with its morning and evening services, Sunday school, choir, and hymnbooks has fallen on hard times. Matt Hannan, a pastor in Vancouver, Wash., offers startling evidence of the decline of the traditional church:

- Eighty to eighty-five percent of churches in North America are plateaued or declining in attendance.

- Approximately 2800 churches close their doors each year.

- Ten million dollars in church property is given away annually by dissolving churches.

- Outflow of people from churches outstrips inflow by a large margin.

- Church growth, where it is seen, is largely transfer growth.[3]

More recent figures are slightly more encouraging. George Barna, a leading researcher, asserts that the average church is growing and that church attendance is up somewhat since 1990.[4] However, he points out that the increase is slight. He further asserts that the average church in America is not outreach-oriented.[5] It seems that many if not most

American churches are barely holding their own.

This contrasts startlingly with the great commission challenge to reach all nations (Matt. 28:19-20). It also contrasts with the church of the New Testament which grew spiritually and numerically. Consider Luke's description of the church at Jerusalem: "praising God and enjoying the favor of all the people. And the Lord added to their number daily those who were being saved" (Acts 2:47) and, "Nevertheless, more and more men and women believed in the Lord and were added to their number" (Acts 5:14). Far from taking the offensive in any great evangelistic effort, most churches seem to be wrestling with the challenge of maintaining their present size or growing slightly. If Hannan's figures are accurate, more than a few are wrestling with the issue of their own survival. Some would argue that numerical growth proves nothing about evangelism. We disagree. If a church is shrinking to the point of concern over its survival, it's a safe bet that evangelism is not taking place. When evangelism occurs, numerical growth usually follows. If numbers demonstrate nothing, why would Luke bother to describe the numerical growth of the church at Jerusalem? Clearly, the stagnant state of many American churches is cause for concern.

The Success of New Models of Ministry

In stark contrast to the pessimistic picture presented by the traditional church in America, new models of ministry are emerging offering alternative approaches to ministry and showing signs of great commission success among baby boomers. These new approaches to church programming and style are creating major changes in the ecclesiastical climate of America. I divide these new models into six types: Seeker-Centered, Seeker-Sensitive, Blended, Multiple Track, Satellite, and Rebirthed.[6]

One of the premier examples of an alternative approach to church is that of Bill Hybels. His now-famous Willow Creek Community Church in South Barrington, Ill., began by finding out all of the things people dislike about traditional church styles and eliminating them. Willow Creek pioneered the seeker-centered model in which the entire worship experience is geared toward making an unchurched person feel more like he is going to a theater than a church. Willow Creek became an "unchurchy" church and a "safe place to hear a dangerous message." From this philosophy has grown a church boasting some 15,000 in weekly attendance, a multimillion-dollar facility and a seven-day-per-week program that educates Christians during the week and reaches "unchurched Harrys" on weekends. This approach has proven so successful in attracting unchurched people, it has spawned many imitators. More than 2,960 churches form the "Willow Creek Association." They are bound together by the philosophy of ministry pioneered by Bill Hybels.[7]

A second new model of ministry is seen in New Hope Community Church of Portland, Ore. Former pastor Dale Galloway built the church on "TLC" or "cell" groups that meet in homes all over the city. More than 500 such groups meet weekly with approximately 5,000 in attendance. More than a home Bible study, Galloway describes TLC groups as foundational to his church. "Cells are not another ministry of the church, cells are the church."[8]

The whole concept of small groups as an expression of the body of Christ is catching on and slowly changing the way American churches function.[9] Churches regularly find that small groups gain greater participation than traditional prayer meetings. These groups also enhance the spiritual health of Christians who "spur one another on to love and good deeds" (Heb. 10:24). So significant is the small group movement that there is a rising number of churches that meet *exclusively* in homes. The "house-church" movement, as it is called, is fueled by the desire for a form of church that stresses a deeper spiritual life and greater interpersonal involvement in an informal and nontraditional setting.[10]

The success of these and other innovative approaches to church life stands in stark contrast to the stagnant realities of many traditional churches in America. No pastor can afford to ignore them. The need for change is evident. Jesus criticized the leaders of Israel saying, "You have a fine way of setting aside the commands of God in order to observe your own traditions!" (Mark 7:9). It is amazing how a cherished tradition can grow in emphasis until it actually stands in the way of fulfilling God's commands. It is more amazing that many will still zealously defend that tradition. Traditions exist today just as in Jesus' day. Some have no useful purpose in fulfilling the great commission. Some actually stand in the way. Yet these traditions all have their defenders. Some Christians apparently believe it is more important to use a King James Bible and 400-year-old hymns than it is to reach twentieth-century Americans with the gospel. Some argue that a "seeker" service in which drama and contemporary music attract unchurched people is actually sinful. Some are so comfortable with church services in which unsaved people are seldom if ever seen that they are actually upset when changes are made which bring in "other kinds of people." The path to change is populated with sacred cows and littered with the trampled bodies of pastors who stampeded them. However, where change succeeds, God often does marvelous things.

The Problem with Change

Change is threatening! Change is hard! Change is chaotic! Anyone who has ever tried to break a habit knows that even such a simple change as quitting smoking or changing one's diet is upsetting. Well-established patterns of behavior must be brought to a screeching, protesting halt and new behaviors and habits must be learned. This is very difficult even when you want the change! If it is this difficult to bring change to one's own life, imagine how difficult it is to bring change to an organization consisting of scores of people, many of whom don't want the change in the first place. It is like pouring new wine into old wineskins. The results can be disastrous.

In addition to this natural resistance to change, there are at least three major obstacles to change unique to today's church. Overcoming these hurdles requires great skill in the art of leadership.

The Multicultural Church

"Do you have experience in cross-cultural ministry?" The chairman of the search committee asked. "Yes," the candidate replied, "I have seniors in my church, and I have teens. If that isn't cross-cultural ministry, I don't know what is!" Obviously, transgenerational ministry is not what the chairman had in mind. Nevertheless, we maintain that every church with a congregation consisting of "builders" (people born prior to 1946), "boomers" (people born from 1946 to 1964), and "busters" or "X'ers" (those born after 1964) has at least three distinct cultures within it. It is not just cross-cultural, it is multicultural. So different are these three generations that it is enormously difficult to minister to all three within the same venue. Why are they different? Much has been written on the subject. In simple terms, each generation grew up in a different world.

Builders grew up with the Great Depression and World War II. These hardships shaped them, giving them certain instinctive values. They tend to trust the government but distrust the economy. They work hard, avoid debt, and save for a rainy day. They grew up without TV. They read.[11]

Boomers grew up in the affluence of the 1950s and '60s. Their views were shaped by an ever expanding economy, Vietnam and the assassination of visionary leaders like John F. Kennedy and Martin Luther King, Jr. Unlike their parents, they learned to trust the economy, but distrust the government. They spend more than they earn. They are less loyal and less committed. They get their information increasingly from images on a screen and less and less from books.[12]

Busters, as those born after 1964 are often called, seem more cynical than their parents. They have grown up in the '70s and '80s. Theirs is a high-tech world of cable TV, video games and interactive technologies. They seem as critical of their parents as their parents were of theirs. However, the criticism focuses on different issues. Listen to the words of a member of Generation X:

> You guys seem to have completely lost sight of the emotional work ethic. You spend all your money on every two-second varnish remover, baldness cure or instant religious salvation that comes on cable after midnight. You are always looking for the easy way out, figuring that it's much simpler to stick a vacuum cleaner in your love handles than to eat right in the first place. Your gnatlike attention span has produced a culture of ideas that is far junkier than any video game we could ever waste an hour playing, and the voracity with which you go through self-help books, celebrity diets and unauthorized biographies shows how little soul you had to start with. You were given everything, and then somehow started to confuse your quest for ideological perfection with self-indulgent laziness.[13]

This generation is cynical, more pragmatic than idealistic, and, in the estimation of many, unreliable. Perhaps the best way to illustrate the difference between these three generations is to look at their approach to authority. A builder tends to obey authority, a boomer tends to question authority, a buster tends to ignore authority.

Today's pastors face the formidable task of creating a church atmosphere conducive to effective ministry for all three groups. Change is a daunting prospect simply because the values and viewpoints of the people in his church vary so greatly. The New Testament model for churches is clearly transgenerational. Ideally, a biblical church features one generation ministering to another. That is why Timothy was told to "give proper recognition to those widows who are really in need" (1 Tim. 5:3). In reciprocal fashion, older women were to train younger women to "love their husbands and children" (Titus 2:4). This kind of honor for one another comes hard to generations that have seen as much change as those who are alive today. There is a natural distrust between generations and a natural tug-of-war when it comes to the style of the service, nature of the programs, and allocation of resources.

Institutionalized Resistance

All institutions are slow when it comes to change. This is a necessary facet of the stability that makes an institution trustworthy. Religious institutions are especially change-resistant. In fact, the church is geared to resist change. Leith Anderson lists six obstacles to change inherent in the church. These include: "focus on [the] institution rather than [on its] purpose [for existence], its "socially self-perpetuating" nature, the tendency of the majority to defer to a vocal minority (i.e., minority rule), excessive reverence for "yesterday's innovator," lack of inclination to take risks, and "unwillingness to suffer pain."[14] To these, we would add a seventh: confusion of form with function.

One of the tasks closest to the heart of established churches is that of guarding the truth. Paul told Timothy that the church is the "pillar and foundation of the truth" (1 Tim. 3:15). Three times Paul urged him to guard what had been entrusted to him (1 Tim. 6:20; 2 Tim. 1:12,14). Paul's reference is to nothing less than the truths of Scripture. Historically, the church has rightly understood that it has a "deposit" which must be guarded at all costs.

The problem is the human tendency to confuse a church's methods with its message. A well-entrenched style, program, or method becomes such an expected part of the ecclesiastical landscape, folks begin to regard it as essential. It becomes nearly as hard to challenge methods, like the venerable altar call or the singing of hymns, as it would be to challenge the virgin birth. Thus we confuse form (ministry style) with function (ministry substance). When methods become our fundamentals, the real reasons behind resistance to change go unexamined. Those who resist change simply dig in their heels, insisting on the importance of forms with which they are familiar. They think they are fighting for faith. In fact, they are often fighting for tradition or preference. Nevertheless, this vocal minority often succeeds in hampering efforts to breathe new life into a church.

Reverend Atlas

Along with ministering across generational cultures and institutionalized resistance, a third obstacle to change in a church is the punishment endured by the one who initiates it. Atlas is a mythical figure who was very strong. However, the thing we notice about Atlas is not that he was strong, but that he carried the whole world on his shoulders. A pastor trying to bring change to a church feels very much like that mythical character. He is the focal point of the debate and often bears the burden of criticism alone. He will take the blame if innovation fails but will also bear the brunt of a certain amount of anger if it succeeds. All of the fears, prejudices, stubbornness, and outright spiritual conflicts that result from significant change inevitably find their way to the pastor. When it comes to change, he is Reverend Atlas bearing a burden few understand.

Ben Patterson lists four contributors to sharp criticism of pastoral leadership: transitions, financial difficulties in the church, projection of one's own fears and troubles onto the pastor causing an over-dependence on him for emotional affirmation, and a "consumer mentality."[15] All of these factors are likely to come into play when the status quo is threatened. At such times, Patterson views pastors as lightning rods who find themselves attracting "criticisms that pulsate with gigawatts of negative energy." They must search for ways to avoid "ecclesiastical electrocution."[16]

Others see such a pastor as a soldier in a war. Fighting to clear the path of obstacles and persuading a reluctant church to follow him down the path while under constant sniper fire from critics gives new meaning to the term "veteran pastor." Speed Leas, author of the landmark book *Church Fights*, lists ten predictable causes of conflict. Of those, seven have to do with change.[17] Resistance to change brings about conflict. In time, conflict discourages pastors and tempts them to quit. The conflict can be fierce, ranging from "level I conflict" (a disagreement that everyone wants to solve) all the way to "level V conflict" (an intractable conflict in which each party supposes the other to be evil).[18] There is no question that the pastor seeking change is in a challenging position. Often the change-agent role challenges men right into another line of work. Our survey found that resistance to change was a contributing cause of resignation for 43% of the pastors surveyed.[19] Clearly, coping with the role of change agent is necessary to survival in the modern pastorate.

Five Approaches to Change

Dealing with the multicultural gridlock of the modern church is a difficult but not impossible task. Many innovative approaches have been employed with varying results. As mentioned previously, I identified six models that can be used effectively in some circumstances.

The Seeker-Centered Model

This approach to church ministry targets the Sunday morning worship service completely to the unchurched person. Bill Hybels' Willow Creek Community Church is the major example of this model of church. With over 15,000 attendees per week, this model is an effective approach in starting a new church. However, it is very difficult to implement in an established church because such a church is already diverse enough that the whole idea of focusing on a target group is likely to be received as "exclusionary."[20]

The Seeker-Sensitive Model

As the name implies, these churches have chosen to keep their church's worship service sensitively open to unchurched individuals. An outstanding example of this kind of church is Saddleback Valley Community Church of Mission Viejo, Calif. Their entire ministry has been geared to reach people like "Saddleback Sam," a composite model based on demographic and sociographic research into the population of Saddleback Valley. The fastest growing Baptist church in history, it has maintained a one-to-three baptism ratio and spawned over thirty new churches.

The Blended Model

The blended church represents an effort to blend traditional with contemporary church culture and keep peace at the same time. This is the approach currently being attempted at Grace Church in Cypress, Calif. They have a choir and praise teams, a piano and synthesizer, orchestral and modern music. This uneasy blend is maintained with difficulty. Prayer is stressed along with strenuous efforts to educate the older church members (builders). Of course, there is a strong appeal to baby boomers and busters. The major problem with this approach is that it is difficult for leaders to have their heart in both worlds. It is also difficult for the congregation. Much diplomacy is required to prevent conflict from becoming serious. This seems to be a temporary solution at best.

The Multiple-Track Model

A multiple-track church is essentially two churches meeting in one church building. Like the blended church, this church centers around the cultural distinctives of two generations. However, unlike the blended church, the optional track church does so by offering separate programs and services for each generation, making little or no effort to bring them together. This approach has the advantage of allowing people to feel completely comfortable with the service they have chosen to attend. There is no need for the churchgoer to adjust to the cultural differences of a different generation. On the other hand, there is less of the transgenerational interaction that New Testament writers considered normal and desirable.

The Satellite Model

Another approach to change is to begin a satellite church. This approach is a lot like the optional-track church with two important differences: First, the satellite church meets in a different location, and second, it develops its own leadership. These are great advantages. It is important to note, however, that this is not simply "church planting." The satellite church remains affiliated with the original church and the two become what Elmer Towns calls "an extended geographical parish church."[21] Turning the satellite church into an independent and autonomous body is always an option. However, the satellite approach has the advantage of pooling resources and promoting a continuing sense of camaraderie and fellowship among Christians of different backgrounds and cultures. A variation of this approach would be to start a culturally different church and allow it to become autonomous when it is ready. This is "mother-daughter church planting."

The Rebirthed Model

The rebirthed church is life from lifelessness. In this approach to change, a dying church is renewed by essentially beginning a new church within it.[22] This approach has met with considerable success in some denominations, which take dying churches in growing areas and breathes life into them. In such cases, the denomination agrees to help a church on the condition that it disband and start over. During the interim period the church turns its property over to the denomination, which renovates and updates the facilities. While this is taking place, a team of church planters meets with the remaining members in homes. Since the church is no longer in existence as a corporate entity, the denomination makes policy. They work with the church planting team to insure that the replanted church will have a viable leadership structure along with programs and ministry style that will succeed in reaching people for Christ. Usually some of the former members drop out during this phase and new leadership emerges. In time, the new church receives the facilities back and moves in under a new name. To the community, it is a brand new and different church. This perception is correct. The denomination retains control until the new church is up and running. This approach has a big advantage over church planting in that it uses existing facilities and a core group of believers to establish a vibrant new church in less time than would otherwise be possible.

Leadership: The Indispensable Quality

The above discussion is not exhaustive, only instructive. There are other approaches to change currently in use.[23] There is one element in common with all approaches to change: leadership. It is not just important. It is indispensable. A recent analysis of methods being employed with success by southern California church planters revealed eight trends. These included: a well-defined and articulated purpose, demographic targeting, culturally relevant programming, aggressive advertising, process or "discipleship" orientation (as compared to a "decision" orientation), team ministry concept, streamlined structure and a lower priority on building.[24] None of these came into being without strong leadership. In every case, the change came about as a result of one man's efforts to effect change. Lyle Schaller sums up the nature of this kind of leadership:

> "You want to know why this congregation changed from growing older and smaller to growing younger and larger?" asked a longtime member from a church that had made that change. "I'll tell you. Our new minister is a real leader and that has made all the difference in the world!"

> A majority of ministers appear to accept the role of a transactional leader or coach or enabler, who focuses on people in general and on individuals in particular. This is appropriate and highly popular in smaller congregations who love gregarious, articulate, person-centered, extroverted, and caring transactional leadership.

By contrast, the transformational leader is driven by a vision of a new tomorrow, wins supporters and followers for that vision, and transforms the congregation. The change from growing older and smaller to growing younger and larger represents radical change, discontinuity, and requires a new set of priorities. It is a transformation. This often is reflected in the comment of the old-timer who observes, "It sure is different here from when I joined thirty years ago."[25]

This kind of leadership presents a formidable challenge to a pastor who is dependent upon the goodwill of the people he leads for his very livelihood. A man must have vision for the future, a grasp of the mechanics of church growth, and an understanding of the politics within his church. He must also possess the personal resolve, tact and firmness to bring it all together. It is a struggle against the enemies of change: tradition, fear, and inertia. Some men succeed. Some don't. Some men just quit.

There is no question that change is hard. It takes a solid leader to negotiate those treacherous waters. There is no room for the faint of heart when change calls for bold visionary leadership. The arena of leadership is the arena in which your pastor struggles. Help him. If the sacred cows are stampeding, get on your horse and help to calm the herd down. Recognize that taking an unpopular stand is much easier when others stand with you. Perhaps many pastors are too faint of heart to attempt change, but many others are simply tired of fighting alone.

You Can Help!

The change agent pastor need not feel alone. You can offer him help in this worthy effort. Your help can mean the difference between spiritual victory for your pastor and church or defeat because the "general" withdrew from the campaign.

1. Help your pastor find support.

Ben Patterson lists three sources of support for pastors in times of lonely leadership: "memorizing comfort," "finding Aaron and Hur," and "the support of family."[26] The memorizing of Scripture is one of the areas for which a pastor could be held accountable. At the very least, you could give him some comforting passages and encourage him to consider memorizing them. Aaron and Hur held up Moses' arms during the battle against the Amalekites (Exod. 17:8-13). Every pastor needs such people who will be his strength when his strength is faltering. Holding up his arms could involve simple encouragement. It could also involve taking some difficult or tedious tasks off his hands. It should always mean holding him up in prayer. Encouraging him to spend more time with his family and extended family can also help to restore perspective.

2. Help him find intellectual and spiritual stimulation.

It is essential for pastors to regularly step back from ministry and plug into a battery charger. You can encourage this process by working to establish adequate funding in your church for conference expenses, books, and continuing education for your pastor. At a minimum, he needs to read some helpful ministry-oriented books and get away for ministry seminars two or three times per year. Failure to develop people for leadership roles is a critical error.[27] One of the biggest mistakes any church can make is to ask a man to lead it into a successful ministry and then refuse to equip him with the tools he needs to do the job. To put a man in that position is to invite mediocrity, frustration, and discouragement.

3. Get involved in the change.

One ex-pastor was approached shortly after his resignation by a younger member. This man was devastated by the prospect that a pastor with fresh ideas promising a new day for a stagnant church was leaving after just a few years on the field. "All of us younger people were solidly with you. I don't think you realize how much support you had!" he exclaimed. "That's right," answered the pastor, "I didn't realize your support because you never showed up at business meetings to vote for my programs!" That pastor experienced effective minority rule. Those who supported him regularly deferred to the vocal "status-quo" minority. If those who wanted change had made some small effort to support it, that pastor might be there today presiding over a new dawn of ministry effectiveness.

–End Chapter Six–

[1]Leith Anderson, Dying for Change (Minneapolis: Bethany House Publishers, 1990), 9.

[2]Howard A. Snyder, The Problem of Wineskins: Church Structure in a Technological Age (Downers Grove, IL: InterVarsity Press, 1975), 16.

[3]Matt Hannan, "Retooling Traditional Churches," lecture presented in "Min 801, Pastors' Symposium, Contemporary Models of Ministry: Reaching Baby Boomers," 15-19 October 1990, Talbot School of Theology, Biola University, La Mirada, CA, class notes, 24.

[4]George Barna, The Barna Report: An Annual Survey of Life-styles, Values and Religious Views, 1992-93: America Renews Its Search for God (Ventura, CA: Regal Books, 1992), 91.

[5]George Barna, Today's Pastors: A Revealing Look at What Pastors Are Saying about Themselves, Their Peers and the Pressures They Face (Ventura, CA: Regal Books, Gospel Light, 1993), 24.

[6]For a complete description of newer models of ministry see Gary L. McIntosh, Make Room for the Boom or Bust: Six New Models for Reaching Three Generations (Grand Rapids: Revell, 1997).

[7]Peter Jennings, "In the Name of God," ABC television broadcast aired 15 March 1995.

[8]Dale Galloway, quoted in Elmer L. Towns, An Inside Look at 10 of Today's Most Innovative Churches: What They're Doing, How They're Doing It & How You Can Apply Their Ideas in Your Church (Ventura, CA: Regal Books, 1992), 76-78.

[9]Rodney J. Dean, lecture presented in "Min 825, Small Groups: An Expression of the Body of Christ," 21-25 October 1991, Talbot School of Theology, Biola University, La Mirada, CA, class notes.

[10]C. Kirk Hadaway, Francis M. DuBose, and Stuart A. Wright, Home Cell Groups and House Churches (Nashville: Broadman Press, 1987), 28-32.

[11]For a full study of the different generations in our churches today see Gary L. McIntosh, Three Generations: Riding The Waves of Change in Your Church (Grand Rapids: Revell, 1995).

[12]Gary L. McIntosh, "Understanding Baby Boomers," lecure presented in "Min 801, Pastor's Symposium, Contemprary Models of Ministry: Reaching baby Boomers," 15-19 October 1990, Talbot School of Theology, Biola University, La Mirada, CA.

[13]Neil Howe and Bill Strauss, 13th Gen (New York: Vintage Books, 1993), 49; quoted in David DeWitt, The Mature Man: Becoming a Man of Impact (Gresham, OR: Vision House, Publishing, 1994), 43.

[14]Anderson, Dying for Change, 110-117.

[15]Ben Patterson, "The Pastor as Lightning Rod," chap. in Who's in Charge? Standing Up to Leadership Pressures, by Leith Anderson, Jack Hayford, and Ben Patterson, Mastering Ministry's Pressure Points series (Sisters, OR: Multnomah Press Books, 1993), 40-41.

[16]Patterson, "The Pastor as Lightning Rod," 40.

[17]Speed B. Leas, "The Ten Most Predictable Times of Conflict," chap. in Mastering Conflict and Controversy, by Edward G. Dobson, Speed B. Leas, and Marshall Shelley, Mastering Ministry series (Portland: Multnomah, Christianity Today, 1992), 110-116.

[18]Speed B. Leas, "The Varieties of Religious Strife," chap. in Mastering Conflict and Controversy, by Dobson, Leas, and Shelley, 85-93.

[19]Pastoral Survey, see appendix.

[20]Jennings, "In the Name of God."

[21]Towns, 10 Innovative Churches, 89.

[22]McIntosh, Make Room for the Boom or Bust.

[23]Towns, 10 Innovative Churches.

[24]Robert L. Edmondson, "New Directions in Church Planting: An Evaluation of Northwest Baptist Home Mission," paper presented in partial fulfillment of the requirements for "Min 801, Pastor's Symposium: Contemporary Models of Ministry, Reaching Baby Boomers," 15-19 October 1990, Talbot School of Theology, Biola University, La Mirada, CA.

[25]Lyle Schaller, Net Results (March 1989), 66; quoted in Anderson, Dying for Change, 188.

26Patterson, "The Pastor as Lightning Rod," 46.

[27]W. Steven Brown, 13 Fatal Errors Managers Make and How You Can Avoid Them (New York: Berkley Books, 1985), 18.

Chapter Seven

Lord, You Keep Him Humble And We'll Keep Him Poor

ONE SIGNIFICANT REASON pastors quit has to do with a subject few pastors wish to discuss: money. Pastors don't choose their profession hoping to get rich. (Anyone who thinks this is a lucrative profession doesn't have all of his oars in the water!) But neither do they expect to be kept poor. Yet because theirs is a "spiritual" career in a non-profit organization, it is difficult for them to communicate their desire for a decent wage.

"How much do you need?" the chairman of the board asked. Pastor Dave Wilson was nonplussed. How does one answer a question like that? It was not the first time he had heard it. Each year the ritual was the same. As the board prepared the budget, they "reviewed" Dave's salary by asking him this question. Each year he didn't know how to answer it. How does one define "need"? He and his family were eating. They had a roof over their heads. They paid their bills on time. On the other hand, they had little money for things like savings, or taking vacations, getting regular dental and eye exams, or replacing their aging car. Were these needs? An objective observer would say, "Yes." Dave Wilson had trouble doing so. He kept thinking of Matt. 6:25, "Therefore I tell you, do not worry about your life, what you will eat or drink; or about your body, what you will wear. Is not life more important than food, and the body more important than clothes?" He also remembered all the old war stories his older colleagues told of desperate times in the ministry. Many older pastors knew what it was to be truly poor. In addition, each of the men on his board was part of the World War II generation. They had known real hardship in their day. Dave didn't want to whine to these men. Besides, this was not a large church and he felt guilty asking for more even though he strongly wished they would offer it to him. "Oh, we're doing all right," he replied feeling dishonest. The board passed a token increase in salary just as they had done each of the past five years. The increase didn't keep pace with inflation. While the church was under the impression that they were increasing Dave's salary regularly, in fact their pastor and his family had less buying power now than when they had begun.

Deep inside, Dave began to resent this careless treatment of issues so vital to his family's well-being. He inwardly kicked himself for not having the courage to speak his mind on the subject. Besides the financial hardship which was becoming acute, there was a sense of professional pain associated with his small salary. Dave felt this in two ways. First, he preached to many men who outearned him by far, men who had worked hard and been rewarded with financial success. While Dave knew that a high salary is not the right way to measure a person's worth, he nevertheless felt a little "out of his league" with these men. They operated at such a different economic level. Dave also felt that his low salary ultimately betrayed the level of value people accorded the church and its pastor. He remembered opening the mail one day shortly after his arrival in the church and discovering a check mailed in by a church member who was traveling. "Tithe" was printed clearly on the memo line. This man was in the refuse business. Few people grow up wanting to do what he did for a living. Yet his tithe check indicated that his salary was exactly double Pastor Dave's. For some reason, Dave had never forgotten that accidental revelation. Today he was fighting off the thought that his church valued their pastor less than society in general values a garbage collector. This thought was followed by another equally distasteful one: "Maybe I should consider another line of work."

God and Mammon: Some Facts About Ministers' Pay

If the Scriptural assertion is true that, "where your treasure is, there your heart will be also" (Matt. 6:21), then most pastors don't have the hearts of their people. By any objective standard, the average pastor is underpaid. The job requires a high level of training and a higher level of commitment. Considering the extraordinary responsibility and sacrifice of time, emotional energy, and privacy in the modern pastorate, the average man in that field earns far less than other professionals with similar levels of training. In 1993, the median salary of all senior pastors was $32,049.[1] This compares with the median annual income for married couple families in the U.S. which was just below $40,000.[2]

It may seem unfair to compare the median salary of one professional group with the median household income for married couples. After all, many married couples rely on not one, but two incomes. However, it is not an unfair comparison. In large numbers of churches, "the pastor's wife is expected not to work but to serve the church in a volunteer [or low wage] capacity" while helping her husband's ministry by being a model homemaker.[3] In such situations, the church sees itself as hiring not just a pastor, but a pastoral couple. Also, a higher-than-average level of training, greater-than-average responsibilities, deeper-than-average commitment, and longer-than-average hours should result in a bigger-than-average salary package. That is not the case when it comes to pastors. In fact, pastors' salaries are well below that of other groups such as "teachers, corporate managers, engineers, and doctors."[4] "About one out of every eight Protestant pastors ... is bivocational."[5] These men work a second job for the privilege of pastoring. The level of experience seems to make little difference in the level of pay. The median salary of the most experienced pastors differs from those just starting out by only about 30% and is still well below that of other professional groups.[6] This problem is getting worse. Statistics indicate that the average pastor's annual salary increases do not keep pace with inflation meaning that, as time goes by, pastors' purchasing power is actually shrinking.[7] Charles Haddon Spurgeon wrote over a hundred years ago, "Ignorant beings they must be if they look for wealth in connection with the Baptist ministry."[8] He is still right.

Why This Discrepancy?

Why does this difference between the salaries of God's servants and those who work in secular vocations exist? There are several reasons. Three different groups of people contribute to the problem. The first is pastors themselves.

The Pastor

Remember how Dave Wilson felt? He didn't want to ask his people for more of their hard-earned money and he didn't want to ask his board for anything. He is certainly not alone. Pastors find it difficult to discuss their financial needs with the leadership board of their church. The reason boils down to fear. "Some pastors fear getting their heads bitten off; others fear the appearance of greed or a lack of contentment. Some fear breaking the spiritual relationship with their board."[9] Whatever the cause, pastors often don't tell the whole story. When a pastor is less than honest with his board about salary issues, he has himself to blame for his financial woes.

The Board

Church boards consist of volunteers—laymen who give their time to help guide the church. There are times when the business affairs of the body suffer because of the amateur makeup of the board. One of those times is when the pastor's salary is under review. Not only is this discussion often shoved to the end of a long administrative meeting,[10] church boards frequently make this major decision without adequate information.

First, the board often doesn't understand what a good salary is for people in the helping professions. One pastor, after several years of frustration over salary issues, finally summoned up courage and broached the subject with one of his board members. The board member encouraged him to write up a brief history of his salary before and after his entrance into ministry, comparing it with that of other professional groups requiring similar education, and adjusting it for inflation. When he presented this information to the board, the members were shocked. They had not even realized that their pastor's salary was far below those in other similar professions. Nor had they realized that, in terms of buying power, their leader now earned *less* than he had in temporary jobs during seminary. This revelation caused them to initiate a series of substantial salary increases to bring his salary into a more realistic range.

Not only do boards lack information on typical salaries in the other helping professions, they also frequently make "apples and oranges" comparisons between their own salaries and that of their pastor. The average paycheck does not reflect the total amount paid by an employer to retain an employee. In addition to wages, an employer covers such expenses as insurance, Social Security contributions, retirement, and other benefits.[11] All of these are part of the "cost of employment." These expenses are real but are often not considered by employees because they are paid out before the paycheck is issued. People often think of their salary as nearly synonymous with the cost of their employment. Certainly few realize that the cost of employment can be as much as 40% higher than the salary. With this mindset, board members determine a pastor's salary package by comparing it with their own. What they don't consider is that much of the overhead which is *paid for them by their employer* must be *paid by their pastor out of his paycheck.* Thus it looks like the pastor is doing better than he is. One church dealt with this by taking out the "cost of employment" items such as professional ministerial expenses, books and subscriptions, mileage, and medical insurance. They placed these in a budget category called "Administration." However, they found that this only partially eliminated the incorrect comparisons.

> Even with these changes, in numerous areas a pastor's salary cannot be compared exactly with a layperson's salary. For instance, few lay people (except military personnel) have anything similar to a tax-exempt housing allowance. Not many lay people understand how it works. Some underestimate its benefits; others vastly exaggerate its worth.
>
> Often lay people also misunderstand self-employment taxes. Since most pastors are self-employed for social security purposes, they pay substantially higher social security taxes than those who work as company employees. Unless a layperson is self-employed, half of his social security taxes are paid by his employer. It's another part of that extra 40 percent that most people forget when figuring their salary.[12]

These misleading comparisons result in the pastor and his family suffering financially while the decision makers are under the false impression that they are paying the pastor well.

The Congregation

The congregation contributes to the problem of low pastoral salaries in various ways too. First and foremost, there is the small size of the average congregation. Church growth researchers have estimated that the average church size in America is 85 to 100.[13] When the church is this small, money is naturally a problem. The pastor must compete for dollars with missionaries, new carpet, and the parking lot paving project.

Many churches also have a vocal financial worrywart. He is the kind who shows up at business meetings with his calculator and says, "No way!" Such people often begrudge the pastor any kind of increase in pay.[14] The influence of even a few such worrisome individuals can make a church very cautious about increasing a pastor's salary.

Sometimes it really does boil down to a lack of value placed on the ministry itself. It has been said that, ultimately, market forces determine salaries.[15] Thus professional sports figures earn unheard of salaries because large numbers of people want their "product." The dollars flow in through ticket sales and advertising fees generated by enthusiastic fans. Where is the enthusiasm of Christians for the gospel ministry? Matthew 6:21 indicates that our heart and our finances follow one another around. If this is the case, then even for a small church the problem usually isn't so much a lack of money as it is a lack of heart for the ministry. If Christians were as enthusiastic about church as the average baseball fan is about his game, perhaps we would be talking about a pastoral salary cap!

So What? The Effect on Pastors

Although many are reluctant to admit it, the effect of low salaries on pastors is devastating. It causes several unfortunate dynamics that combine to frustrate the pastor and ultimately the ministry itself. These include constant financial pressures which make a man work less effectively,[16] pressure to live a similar lifestyle to the people in the church in spite of limited means, and a lack of avenues by which to increase one's income.[17] These pressures make a pastor and his family feel trapped, isolated, and desperate the kind of feelings that lead to a departure from ministry. Our research indicates that nearly one-third of all pastors who resign do so in part because of financial pressure.[18] Churches, on the other hand, seem largely unaware of this problem. Only 13% cited salary issues as a factor in their last pastor's decision to resign.[19] Other research seems to bear out these findings.[20]

It isn't just the financial pressure, it is the sense of low esteem represented by the low salary that hurts many men.

> The respect a parish has for its minister can mean the difference between a dynamic or a defeated church leadership. The willingness or unwillingness of a congregation to meet adequately the pastor's physical needs affects how a pastor feels about his ministry and his sense of worth. The church members' sense of stewardship is transmitted through him—self-respect and appreciation—or quite the opposite.
>
> Distressingly, the oft-repeated phrase, "Where your treasure is, there will your heart be also," (Matt. 6:21 RSV) continues to be in stiff competition with the old saw, still in the consciousness of

a majority of church members, "Lord, you keep him humble—we'll keep him poor."[21]

Consider the true story of a pastor and his family who in spite of an advanced degree and a medium-sized church were forced to accept welfare.

Picture your pastor standing in line for food stamps. It does happen. Many clergy today find it necessary to receive government assistance to feed their families; I am one of them.

I'm a full-time pastor of an upper-middle-class church of 300 members in a mainline denomination. I have a B.A. degree in psychology and a master of divinity degree from a major seminary. I've been married twelve years and have two children. I have committed my life to Christ.

Yet the government has to supplement my income by providing food stamps as well as the Earned Income Credit, which comes through my income taxes, and the free lunch program that my daughter receives in the public school.

How can this be? Even though lay people attempt to do all they can to alleviate world suffering, they often allow their pastors to subsist on the lowest level of income possible.

My wife and I were once able to say we earned everything we received. We worked hard and were paid accordingly. In the ministry it's different. I work all available hours as the "pastor in charge." Whether I work forty hours or eighty hours I receive the same salary, even though I might drive twice the number of miles and spend twice as much for expenses. The harder I work, the more unreimbursed expenses I incur.

Maybe you think my wife should work outside the home. But our children are small, and with the strains of parsonage life, we believe they need their mother's presence.

Somehow it all seems wrong. The pastor should be free to serve God and the people who need him without having to fight the depressing battle of staying alive financially. The pastor's children should not have to grow up in such stark contrast to the lifestyles of the children whose church he serves. They should not have to be "second-class" citizens.

If those who are lay leaders in the churches would give thought to this social problem of the twentieth-century pastor, improvements would be made. The expenses of the ministry are higher than ever and should come out of the church's treasury. The members should sincerely try to determine what their pastor's family needs in the way of financial support. What is your pastor doing without? More important, what is his family doing without? Are his children growing up with a good impression of the church's love and care? Will they be able to receive the necessary education to cope in an increasingly technological world? Is your pastor eligible for welfare?[22]

Fortunately, current statistics indicate that such extreme cases are not common. However, many of the feelings experienced by this pastor are common among ministers earning inadequate salaries. This constant pressure brings with it a very real temptation to leave the ministry altogether.

The Biblical Way

There are those who read the pastoral qualification, "not a lover of money" (1 Tim. 3:3), combine it with verses about stewardship, and come to the conclusion that a church ought to be stingy with their pastor's salary. Not only is this a big leap in logic, but such thinking goes against the clear teaching of Scripture. "The Lord has commanded that those who preach the gospel should receive their living from the gospel" (1 Cor. 9:14), and, "The elders who direct the affairs of the church well are worthy of double honor, especially those whose work is preaching and teaching. For the Scripture says, 'Do not muzzle the ox while it is treading out the grain,' and 'The worker deserves his wages'" (1 Tim. 5:17-18). The phrase "double honor" in this context refers both to honor and financial provision. It does not suggest that the pastor actually be paid twice what others in his line of work earn, but that he be considered worthy of it if he does his work well. The idea is that a church should respect and care for a pastor in an *"ample"* way.[23] Ironically, those who withhold a reasonable salary from a pastor on the grounds that he is not to be a lover of money may be demonstrating their own love for money. James indicts those who pay stingy wages and strongly suggests that it has been their own greed at the heart of the matter. "Look! The wages you failed to pay the workmen who mowed your fields are crying out against you! The cries of the harvesters have reached the ears of the Lord Almighty!" (James 5:4).

One cannot paint all churches or church members with the same brush when it comes to the motives involved in determining pastoral salaries. Still, it is important to understand that paying a pastor what he deserves is not an option. Scripture clearly and repeatedly commands this: "Give everyone what you owe him: If you owe taxes, pay taxes; if revenue, then revenue; if respect, then respect; if honor, then honor" (Rom. 13:7).

Beyond the matter of simple obedience to God, paying a pastor well is good for the church. No pastor who is preoccupied with financial survival can concentrate effectively on his ministry in the church. Listen to the words of Ted Engstrom:

> Often the difference between "winning" and "getting by" for the senior executive is a cost of less than one percent of the organization's income. But not taking care of the senior executive adequately affects ninety-nine percent of the group's identity and effectiveness. Once your senior executive is "winning" in his personal finances, he can release his entire energy and potential to helping the group succeed—a great energy release for a relatively few dollars.

> The financial compensation to the senior executive is critical to his effectiveness as your directional leader...

> *Note: Verbally expressing appreciation is critical to a senior executive's motivation, but it cannot take the place of compensation.*[24]

A wise church seeks to remove money as a preoccupation for their pastor. "If we have an effective pastor and we aren't willing to pay him fairly for his work, we'll probably lose him to a church that will."[25] Many pastors leave the ministry entirely because they simply cannot make ends meet.[26] If a church pays its pastor in accordance with scriptural guidelines and attitudes, it will remove one major obstacle to his remaining there.

Churches, not only pastors, benefit when their pastors are paid appropriately. Allow God to bless you for your generosity. "A generous man will prosper; he who refreshes others will himself be refreshed" (Prov. 11:25). There is no command in Scripture to err on the side of caution when it comes to generosity. In this particular area, a little generosity could return to you ten-fold by giving you a more effective and longer-lasting pastor. If you don't relish the idea of going through yet another pastoral transition, this is one area where a penny's worth of prevention could save you a dollar's worth of cure.

You Can Help!

This is a critical issue. A church needs to address this matter if it wishes to retain its pastor for a long time. There are several ways that you can help as a church.

1. Realize what is at stake.

Few would argue that losing a pastor is good for the church. With a few exceptions, a pastorless church waits on hold until a new pastor comes on board then suffers through a time of adjustment before he becomes an effective leader. If the new man stays the average four years, there is precious little progress being made. It simply takes longer than that for a man to effectively make a mark on a church. Remember, any pastorate of less than seven years may be "cost-*inef-*fective."[27] Paying pastors adequately can spell the difference between having one around long enough to effectively lead, or experiencing a continual turnover that prevents effective leadership from ever taking place.

2. Pay the pastor on the basis of worth not need.

Don't ask him "How much do you need?" Not only is that question almost impossible to answer, it represents the wrong basis for determining a pastor's salary. I Timothy doesn't say "double what he needs." On the contrary, it commands double honor for a job well done! Biehl and Engstrom suggest several factors to take into consideration when paying a senior executive. Seven of them can be applied to the pastor as well:

1. time in position
2. value and level of the position
3. record of performance
4. cost of living
5. bonus
6. housing allowance
7. expense account, especially for personal growth and organizational entertaining[28]

Obviously, the process of determining a pastor's compensation should be a bit more sophisticated than just asking, "How much do you need?"

3. Find ways to eliminate "apples and oranges" comparisons.

As noted earlier, such comparisons invariably do the pastor a disservice. Here are several ways to insure that your church considers the pastor's salary in its proper light. First, consider changing your budget reports to show "cost of ministry" items such as professional and auto expenses, insurance, books and subscriptions in a category separate from that of the pastor's salary. These are not compensation. They represent the cost of employment for a pastor. Perhaps they should be labeled "Administration."[29] Since he pays a higher rate for Social Security, you should consider putting half of this under "Administration" as other employers do. Second, appoint two or three qualified people to act as a salary review committee.[30] They should carefully examine the pastor's compensation package, taking into consideration all seven of the factors listed above, and carefully considering the unique facets of his financial status such as the tax-exempt housing allowance and the higher self-employment rate for Social Security. They should then recommend a salary level that is realistic and in keeping with scriptural admonitions. The process should take place once a year. Third, consider making the pastor's salary confidential.[31] This may not be practical in a smaller church with a solo pastor. But in a multistaff church (or even one with a paid secretary), the salaries can appear together on one line of a financial report. This is not for the purpose of hiding or confusing anyone. It is simply a way of keeping unfair comparisons to a minimum.

4. Read the helpful manual, "How To Develop A Pastoral Compensation Plan."

Dr. Gary L. McIntosh has written a practical, easy to use manual to assist local churches in designing a pastoral compensation package. It includes an overview of the relevant biblical passages, insight in the four major models for paying pastors, and a specific compensation model for a church to follow. In addition complete information on organizing a year-end review of the pastoral salary is included. Information on reimbursements, benefits, and base salaries, along with insights on paying a multiple staff, makes this manual one of the most complete. (Available from ChurchSmart Resources: 1-800-253-4276)

–End Chapter Seven–

[1]George Barna, Today's Pastors: <u>A Revealing Look at What Pastors Are Saying about Themselves, Their Peers and the Pressures They Face</u> (Ventura, CA: Regal Books, Gospel Light, 1993), 37.

[2]Data from the Bureau of Labor Statistics, 1992; quoted in Barna, Today's Pastors, 39.

[3]Barna, <u>Today's Pastors</u>, 39.

[4]Barna, <u>Today's Pastors</u>, 37.

[5]Barna, <u>Today's Pastors</u>, 39.

[6]Barna, <u>Today's Pastors</u>, 39.

[7]<u>Current Thoughts and Trends</u>, May 1992; quoted in H. B. London, Jr. and Neil B. Wiseman, <u>Pastors at Risk: Help for Pastors, Hope for the Church</u> (Wheaton, IL: Victor Books, Scripture Press Publications, 1993), 127.

[8]C. H. Spurgeon, <u>Lectures to My Students</u> (Grand Rapids: Zondervan Publishing House, 1980), 27.

[9]Larry W. Osborne, "Negotiating a Fair Salary," <u>Leadership Journal</u> 8, no. 1 (Winter 1987): 86.

[10]Osborne, "Negotiating a Fair Salary:" 86.

[11]Osborne, "Negotiating a Fair Salary:" 87-88.

[12]Osborne, "Negotiating a Fair Salary:" 88.

[13]Matt Hannan, "Retooling Traditional Churches," lecture presented in "Min 801, Pastors' Symposium, Contemporary Models of Ministry: Reaching Baby Boomers," 15-19 October 1990, Talbot School of Theology, Biola University, La Mirada, CA. class notes, 12.

[14]Wayne Pohl, "Setting Staff Salaries," chap. in <u>Mastering Church Finances</u>, by Richard L. Bergstrom, Gary Fenton, Wayne A. Pohl, Mastering Ministry series (Sisters, OR: Multnomah Press, Christianity Today, 1992), 155.

[15]Rush Limbaugh, EIB Network radio broadcast, 2 March 1995.

[16]Pohl, "Setting Staff Salaries," 154.

[17]London and Wiseman, <u>Pastors at Risk</u>, 113-114.

[18]Pastoral Survey, see appendix.

[19]Church Survey, see appendix.

[20]David Goetz, "Is the Pastor's Family Safe at Home?" <u>Leadership Journal</u> 13, no. 4 (Fall 1992): 38-44.

[21]Lucille Lavender, <u>They Cry, Too! What You Always Wanted to Know about Your Minister but Didn't Know Whom to Ask</u> (New York: Hawthorn Books, W. Clement Stone, 1976), 68.

[22]Eternity, September 1980: 65; quoted in Henry A. Virkler, <u>Choosing a New Pastor: The Complete Handbook</u> (Nashville: Oliver Nelson, Thomas Nelson, 1992), 120-121.

[23]Ralph Earle, "1 Timothy," in The Expositor's Bible Commentary: With The New International Version of The Holy Bible, vol. 11, ed. Frank E. Gaebelein (Grand Rapids, MI: Regency Reference Library, Zondervan Publishing House, 1978), 380.

[24]Bobb Beihl and Ted W. Engstrom, Increasing Your Boardroom Confidence (Sisters, OR: Questar Publishing, 1988), 195.

[25]Virkler, Choosing a New Pastor, 123.

[26]London and Wiseman, Pastors at Risk, 115.

[27]Kennon L. Callahan, Twelve Keys to an Effective Church: Strategic Planning for Mission (San Francisco: Harper & Row, Publishers, 1983), 51.

[28]Biehl and Engstrom, Increasing Your Boardroom Confidence, 195.

[29]Osborne, "Negotiating a Fair Salary," 88.

[30]Virkler, Choosing a New Pastor, 124.

[31]Pohl, "Setting Staff Salaries," 162.

Chapter Eight

FRIEND OR FLOCK?

"TRANSCONTINENTAL CONGREPHOBIA: the feeling, even when you're 1800 miles from home, that one of your parishioners is eavesdropping in the next booth."[1]

We laughed as we read the cartoon caption and can still see the picture: a young pastor and his family dressed casually, glancing furtively about in fear that spies from the church have followed them on vacation. This cartoon reminds us of Tony's resignation from Valley Church (chapter 1). Tony resented the need to be a friend to people who were often unappreciative. "I got tired of acting as if I liked people that I really couldn't stand," he said.

The relationship between a pastor and his people is unique. It has special rewards but also special hardships. Is it professional or personal? It's both—and neither. It is a professional relationship made less so by the presence of personal considerations. It is a personal relationship made less so by the presence of professional constraints. A pastor may be a friend to many and yet have no friends. He can walk among the crowd and be its center of attention, a master of ceremonies, and exemplar of virtue, and yet be alone. Our survey of pastors found that feelings of loneliness and isolation figured into a decision to resign in nearly one out of three instances.[2] It is difficult for anyone who hasn't been a pastor to grasp the isolation imposed by the professional constraints of that office. However, we can learn how to help prevent it.

Wanted: A Professional/Personal/Pastoral Friend

One expectation churches have of most pastors is friendship. The pastor must "preach the word and love the people." This is sometimes a tough task.

> These men are expected to be a friend to everyone—*but few are friends to them*. It is easy to love the lovable. Your pastor, more than anyone, is asked to be a friend to and love the unlovable.

Jesus spoke strongly of this: "And whenever a village [a church member?] won't accept you or listen to you, shake off the dust from your feet as you leave; it is a sign that you have abandoned it to its fate." (Mark 6:11 LB).

This is plain talk from the Lord.

"You have done what you could," he is saying. "Don't waste your energies with those who will have none of it. Utilize your time and energies to better advantage on those who really want to hear about God's love for them. God loves the others, too, but they've had their chance."

Today's pastor faces a dilemma. Should *he* give up on them? Ministers spend needless time and energy on Christian believers who are unlovable and do not want to change. Where does the pastor go when he needs a friend to help him get his priorities and perspectives back?[3]

Fortunately, the task of loving people is not always onerous. In fact it is not usually so. What makes it difficult is that this task is a requirement of an office, part of a job description. These are not naturally developed relationships. Rather, they are expected *based on the office of the pastorate*. The pastor is a *professional friend*. A longtime member of a church decided to drop his membership and begin worshipping with a different congregation. He had various complaints. The services were too contemporary. The preaching missed the mark. As he discussed his misgivings, it became apparent that behind them was the pain of personal disappointment in his pastor. He had expected to develop a close friendship with his pastor. When this expectation went unfulfilled, he became disillusioned with the pastor's whole ministry and dropped out. Had he considered the ramifications of such an expectation, he might have realized that it was unrealistic. No pastor can have that kind of relationship with everyone. However, he is not alone. Such expectations are common.

In addition to being a *professional friend*, the minister must occupy the role of *pastor* with those whom he befriends. He is not simply a friend, but an evangelist, a discipler, a manager, a counselor, a comforter, a dispenser of spiritual wisdom and inspiration, and, in the emotional framework of some congregants, a kind of surrogate father.[4]

Is it unreasonable to expect a pastor to occupy the role of pastor? No. However, expecting him to be both pastor and buddy at the same time may be. The role of pastor and the role of friend sometimes are very different. We find that people act differently around us when they know that we are a pastor. That role imposes constraints on everyone. It is difficult for a pastor to have a satisfying relationship with someone who is on his best behavior in the presence of his minister. Similarly, it is difficult for the minister to relax because his friend expects him to act like a pastor. I recall an incident which illustrates this well. While candidating for a church, I was told that the people wanted a pastor who would "just be himself." After pastoring the church for several months, I was at a board member's home when the board member called from the across the living room, "Pastor, throw me a cookie!" Joining in the fun, I picked up a cookie and jokingly tossed it across the room to the church member. At the time everyone in the room laughed. But, later in the evening after everyone had gone home, the board member who had asked me to throw him a cookie verbally attacked me saying, "I can't believe my pastor would throw a cookie in my house."

When a pastor tries to develop friendship with a parishioner, the result is a tense relationship—*a professional <u>pastoral</u> friendship*. It is a friendship made less intimate by the presence of pastoral constraints and duties. To the parishioner, the minister is not only his friend, but also his *pastor*. To the pastor, the parishioner is not only his friend, but also a member of his church. The pastor is on the job whenever they are together. One unfortunate consequence of this pastoral persona is that the pastor often cannot admit to his own humanity.

> Who do ministers turn to when they are in trouble?

> Much, if not most, of the difficulty here lies with the attitude. Of course, ministers are free to get help if they need it. They are as free as anyone. The problem lies in an unreal role image sometimes fostered by lay persons and accepted by many ministers. Ministers are helpers. They are not supposed to need help. People go to ministers to receive counsel. Ministers know all about these things. They know how to deal with problems, for they work with peoples' problems all the time. Surely, if anything goes wrong in their own lives, they know what to do about it. It's their job to know.[5]

A pastor may desperately need help with his own problems, but he feels he must hide this need and continue to play the role of the general expert on life, the *professional pastoral friend*, twenty-four hours a day, no matter where he is.

> Because the community of faith calls the pastor to be its official representative, the clergy find themselves in a double bind. At a practical level, they are expected to be moral examples of high Christian living and, unlike the laity, they are also called to a formal and official accountability to the Christian community. This essentially contractual agreement implies that for the clergy no official spiritual difference exists between the life lived while "on duty" and one's private life.[6]

There is certainly nothing wrong with expecting a pastor to hold to high spiritual standards. He must be a virtuous person, not just act like one when "on duty." This is scriptural. There is, however, something very wrong with expecting him to do pastoral work at any and all hours whether urgent or not. Many people seem to forget the obvious: pastoral work is, after all, work.

A pastoral acquaintance recently told us that he is disgusted with the way his people regularly invade his private time. His family maintains a weekly "game night." On one such night recently, they set up the games on the living room floor as usual. They were just starting to play and relax when the doorbell rang. One of the church leaders walked in unannounced along with his wife. It was obvious that their pastor was busy with his own family. Not only did this fail to deter the intrusive couple, they didn't even seem to notice. If it had been an emergency the pastor would have understood, but they just wanted to air their opinions about another couple going through a painful divorce. This was not what that pastor had in mind for family night.

No one can be permanently "on duty." Overidentification with one's job is a common failing leading to burnout.[7] In the pastorate, overidentification with the job is not just encouraged, it is practically canonized. A pastor is regularly called upon to be more than just a *professional pastoral friend*. He must be a *professional and personal pastoral friend*. It is not just a nine-to-five career role which is required, but a life. It is not just professional; it is personal. There is no separation between the two. The pastor must maintain this *professional/personal/pastora* persona at all times. His job as currently conceived involves being a pastor and friend to any who need him at any time.

Results of the Professional/Personal/ Pastoral Persona

There are three inevitable results of the professional/personal/pastoral persona. First, in the church, *every relationship is a pastoral relationship*. The pastor has no ordinary friends in his church. He sustains a professional and pastoral role with all of them. There may be friendship, but it is always subject to the constraints of the pastoral role. Many older texts on pastoral ministry, such as this one by Charles Haddon Spurgeon, suggest that this is a necessary reality:

> *Our position in the church will also conduce to this.* A minister fully equipped for his work will usually be a spirit by himself, above, beyond, and apart from others. The most loving of his people cannot enter into his peculiar thoughts, cares, and temptations. In the ranks, men walk shoulder to shoulder, with many comrades, but as the officer rises in rank, men of his standing are fewer in number. There are many soldiers, few captains, fewer colonels, but only one commander-in-chief. So, in our churches, the man who the Lord raises as a leader becomes, in the same degree in which he is a superior man, a solitary man. The mountain-tops stand solemnly apart, and talk only with God as He visits their terrible solitudes.[8]

Spurgeon magnified his office suggesting that the reality of isolation is a function of the superiority of the one in the office. Ralph G. Turnbull, noted pastoral author, wrote that loneliness is a natural result of the nature of pastoral duties.

> The minister has responsibilities which force him into a lonely position. As he engages in these he finds himself alone. He is a pastor and thus will seek to shepherd the flock. Loneliness is inescapable and the pastor has his share. His lot is such that he is a man among men and yet a man set apart. His office and its function tend to isolate him, if not in a physical sense, in a spiritual way. His thoughts and brooding over the life and work of his congregation produce a feeling of loneliness.[9]

In either case the reality is the same. A pastor is alone amidst the people he befriends. He knows and is known, but what he knows and what is known of him are all influenced by his title: Pastor.

Second, *every pastoral relationship is influenced more by pastoral expectations than by personal preference*. The pastor is expected to be friendly to everyone, rejecting no one. He must be polite at all times and never respond in kind to any nasty barb a church member throws his way. "The local butcher can tell off an annoying old busy body. Not so the man of God."[10] This constraint upon his reaction to negative situations was humorously described by Garrison Keillor. He said of his mythical friend Pastor Inkvest, "When he hit his knee on the corner of a desk drawer, his choice of language was limited and didn't include all the most satisfying stuff."[11] These expectations influence his demeanor with all his parishioners. Even friendships that might otherwise develop naturally feel less than genuine because they did not form on the basis of personal choice, but of expectation.

What the people know of the pastor is influenced by his "pastoral facade," and what he knows of the people is influenced by their natural reticence to let their hair down in front of the pastor. Although pastors strive to be themselves, the need to maintain a certain pastoral bearing is never absent. It influences all relationships, subtly changing their character so that the relationship is not friend to friend, but shepherd to sheep. The pastor has no choice in this. It is inevitable. Thus, he may feel like a slave to his role, wishing for the intimacy of genuine friendship but always sensing the pastoral barrier.

Third, *pastoral relationships are a pastor's main relationships*. Remember, he is not just a pastor when he is doing church business, but all of the time. The idea that he could have a life outside of the pastoral role is quite foreign to many parishioners. Boyd Stoltz pastored a rural church. His situation was unique in that he already lived in the area, albeit in town thirty-five miles from the church. Many in the church assumed that he would sell his home and move to the town in which the church was located. When instead it became apparent that he intended to commute, some of the church members were unhappy. There were many who had expected his involvement in the social and even political life of their community. They had similar expectations of his wife and children. They believed Boyd's pastoral role encompassed all of his life and that of his family during most of their waking hours. Because he was on the church payroll, many assumed the church had broad powers to dictate his personal choices. This was a theory in need of puncturing. His firm decision to maintain a private life let at least some of the air out of it. Nevertheless, in spite of living some distance from the church building, the Stolzes still struggle to develop a social life outside of the church. Although they live in another community, the ministry absorbs them. Boyd's professional life eclipses his social life. He and his wife are occasionally lonely. Our survey indicates that the Stolzes' experience is not unique. Among respondents, 30% said that loneliness was a part of their decision to resign from their church.[12]

When a pastor has all his friends in his church, he has no friends. As much as his people may care for him and he for them, they are not friends in the normal sense of that word. He is to them a professional/personal/pastoral friend. The relationship is defined by his job as pastor.

Wanted: A Friend

Human beings need friendship. God designed us for this. "It is not good for the man to be alone" (Gen. 2:18a). Ben Patterson describes the need for friendship which he experienced deeply at a discouraging time in ministry.

> I felt completely alone. Sure, many people in the church loved and supported me, but I couldn't think of one person in that fellowship who was a close friend. I didn't have one person with whom I could safely, honestly be me, the real me—tears, fears, clay feet and all.[13]

It is our belief that a well-balanced life for a pastor includes some social arena in which the pastor can safely discard his pastoral image, if only for a while.

> The most important benefits of friendship are: emotional encouragement, help in trouble, personal stability, spiritual help and counsel, freedom of expression, protection from loneliness and isolation, love and acceptance, and opportunities to give ourselves to others.... Some healthy motives for building friendships are: to be built up personally, to grow spiritually, to give to another person, to have a mentor, and to be encouraged.[14]

One pastor experiencing chest pains entered a hospital. As he lay in the hospital bed with heart monitors beeping and doctors conferring all around him, he was uncertain about his condition. Was he having a heart attack? Would he live? Would he die? Suddenly a hospital chaplain appeared and asked if she could pray with him. He automatically put on his pastoral hat, explaining that he was a minister and someone else probably needed her comfort more than he. Her response was to set aside her own pastoral demeanor. She looked around and said in conspiratorial tones, "Pastors need comfort too." It was true. Tears came to his eyes. That simple touch of friendship from a colleague greatly encouraged him. It turned out that his heart pains were not serious. It was a good thing, too. A few minutes later, while the verdict on his heart was still out, the phone by the bed rang. It was one of the church leaders. After asking briefly about his pastor's condition, he launched into a discussion of church problems. If the pastor had been experiencing serious coronary problems, that phone call might have triggered a massive heart attack. As it was, he merely had a vivid demonstration of the great difference which often exists between friend and flock.

If a pastor has adequate emotional support, he can serve well and indefinitely even in difficult circumstances. On the other hand, if he lacks emotional support because all of his relationships are pastoral relationships, even a positive situation can drain him to the point of exhaustion. He needs friends, not just a flock.

You Can Help!

Your pastor needs to be a human being. He needs to accept his own needs and allow others to support him just as he supports others. Bob's son recently asked him if pastors have their own pastors. Bob responded, "They should." His son's quick reply was, "God is your pastor." While this is quite biblical (Ps. 23:1), pastors need care from other humans. In this area, you can help.

1. Offer relational support.

While no relationship within the church is free of the constraint of the pastoral role, some relationships are closer than others. If you enjoy a close relationship with your pastor, learn to empathize with him. Let him know that you are not surprised or disappointed by his humanity. If you are not especially close, you can still support your pastor relationally by encouraging his involvement with you in recreation and diversion.

2. Honor your pastor's need for privacy.

This means keeping church business inside office hours as much as possible, guarding his days off, and making sure he gets away from time to time. It also means that his personal decisions (the car he drives, his wife's choices in clothing, etc.) are personal decisions.

3. Don't begrudge him his friendships.

No one can sustain close friendships with everyone. For pastors, there are also inherent difficulties with friendships in church life. If the pastor has an outside social life and friendships with others that are closer than with you, recognize that this is entirely reasonable and healthy.

4. Encourage his involvement in extracurricular activities such as sports or hobby clubs.

Express your encouragement in this area as based on his needs, not the need to meet people for the sake of evangelism or ministry. While these may well result, he needs to have relationships where he can be himself without concern for professional performance.

–End Chapter Eight–

[1]Doug Hall, cartoon in Leadership Journal 8, no. 2 (Spring 1987): 19.

[2]Pastoral Survey, see appendix.

[3]Lucille Lavender, They Cry, Too! What You Always Wanted to Know about Your Minister but Didn't Know Whom to Ask (New York: Hawthorn Books, W. Clement Stone, 1976), 51-52.

[4]Ben Patterson, "The Pastor as Lightning Rod," chap. in Who's in Charge? Standing Up to Leadership Pressures, Mastering Ministry's Pressure Points series (Sisters, OR: Multnomah Press Books, 1993), 41.

[5]Ray W. Ragsdale, The Mid-Life Crises of a Minister (Waco, TX: Word Books, 1978), 20.

[6]Paul A. Mickey and Ginny W. Ashmore, Clergy Families: Is Normal Life Possible? (Grand Rapids, MI: Zondervan Publishing House, Harper Collins, 1991), 85.

[7]Stanley J. Modic, "Surviving Burnout: The Malady of Our Age," Industry Week, 20 February 1989: 34.

[8]C. H. Spurgeon, Lectures to My Students (Grand Rapids: Zondervan Publishing House, 1980), 157.

[9]Ralph G. Turnbull, A Minister's Obstacles (Flemming H. Revell, 1965), 113-116; quoted in Charles U. Wagner, The Pastor: His Life and Work (Schaumburg, IL: Regular Baptist Press, 1976), 29.

[10]Louis McBurney, Every Pastor Needs a Pastor (Waco, TX: Word Books, 1977), 65.

[11]Garrison Keillor, "The News from Lake Wobegon."

[12]Pastoral Survey, see appendix.

[13]Ben Patterson, "Must Leaders Be Lonely?" chap. in Who's in Charge? by Anderson, Hayford, and Patterson, 154.

[14]Jerry and Mary White, Friends and Friendship: The Secrets of Drawing Closer (Colorado Springs, CO: NavPress, 1982), 50.

Chapter Nine

The Puller Of Strings

A COMMON THREAD runs through all of the discouraging and debilitating issues that tempt pastors to resign: all of them do spiritual harm to him and to the church. This is more than mere coincidence. There is an unseen hand here—a puller of strings. Our adversary, the devil, is bent on destroying pastors and their churches. To recognize this truth, one need only observe the consistency with which spiritual problems arise in churches and often the frequency with which they arise in the same church.

Some time ago, Bob sat in a restaurant talking shop with one of his colleagues. They had been discussing the relative health of various churches with which they were both familiar. Bob became intrigued by his friend's evaluation of a particularly troubled church: "That church has a decades-long history of getting to a certain size and then splitting. The pastor leaves, they spend a year getting another one, and then they do it all over again."

"What accounts for that?" Bob asked, trying to understand the dynamics that create such an entrenched pattern of conflict.

"I don't know," was the frank admission. "The issues are different and the people are different, but the pattern is definite." Filing that discussion away for future reference, Bob began to think about it again when another colleague discussed his ministry with him over a cup of coffee. His church was involved in an intractable and thorny dispute.

A falling out between two individuals had escalated to the point that it became an open wound in the body. People were choosing sides. Battle lines were being drawn. Although the leadership of the church was not involved in the original conflict, their efforts to intervene and bring resolution were like "seizing a dog by the ears" (Prov. 26:17). The situation nearly got out of hand and was resolved only with the loss to that church of several families. Some time after the conflict, Bob asked his friend if he thought that there were any underlying spiritual issues feeding the dispute. After some reflection, he came up with four. First, there was a consistent lack of honor for one another along with a pointed lack of respect for or trust in leadership. Second, there was a carelessness about the application of scriptural principles that manifested itself in various telling ways. Third, there was a huge element of old-fashioned gossip. Some of it was apparently malicious. Finally, the church leadership had lacked the courage to take any public position on various relevant issues because such positions might prove unpopular. As it turned out, those underlying spiritual issues were no secret. They had given the church a mixed reputation in that community for many years.

In an important sense, many of the frequent battles in that church may not have really been about the things that people had supposed. In each case, there might have been little or no conflict at all if the underlying spiritual issues had been addressed by the people involved. The long history of conflict that that church experienced was also likely the result of unresolved spiritual issues.

Viewed from a spiritual perspective, these kinds of ongoing battles take on a different significance, especially when one realizes that the same basic problems have often been at the root of conflicts involving different people and situations for many years and sometimes generations.

One can begin to see the manipulative hand of the evil one. Like a puppeteer, he works unseen. He pulls strings that are invisible to the undiscerning. He influences the thoughts and actions of well-intentioned people as surely as if they were his marionettes. The result is a bizarre show—a kind of puppet allegory in which the exaggerated discord between people is only a figure, a metaphor of sorts speaking loudly and distractingly of the conflict of the day, but softly and cryptically of the real issues.

Churches make serious, even desperate, efforts to deal with these conflicts when they occur, but their efforts often fall short. Perhaps this is because churches often fail to recognize the true nature of the show and who is running it. They fail to resist the devil—the puller of strings. Thus, churches often move from one conflict to another without recognizing the pattern of underlying spiritual issues.

This not-so-subtle pattern has telling effects on a pastor. He pays a heavy price in sleepless nights, recriminations, and resistance to his efforts to lead the church. This is often a major factor in his decision to seek a different position. According to our survey, corporate spiritual defeat plays a role in nearly half of pastoral resignations.[1]

126

What Does the Bible Say?

The reality of spiritual conflict shouldn't surprise us. Scripture makes no secret of it. Nevertheless, it is helpful to remind ourselves of four basic biblical facts.

There Is a Devil

The devil is real. He is not just a force or the personification of evil. He is a personal being possessed of intellect, emotions, and will. "He who does what is sinful is of the devil," wrote John, "because the devil has been sinning from the beginning. The reason the Son of God appeared was to destroy the devil's work" (1 John 3:8). John indicates that the devil has been making moral choices (the wrong ones), and has been doing "work" that the Son of God came to destroy. This is not a description of an impersonal force, or of evil in general. This is a description of a live personal being who is a committed opponent of God. The Bible everywhere uses similar language to describe him. "The term 'devil' signifies 'slanderer.' He slanders God before men, and men before God (Gen. 3:1; Rev. 12:10). His personality is also revealed in the description of the 'man of sin' as 'he that opposeth and exalteth himself against ... God.'"[2] Isaiah 14 and Ezekiel 28 hint at the origin of the devil. A full treatise on the subject is beyond the purpose of this chapter. What is important is that, in speaking of the devil, we are speaking of a living being whose existence and work have profound implications for believers. He is not just a figurative character created by the writers of Scripture to make a point or motivate people. Nor is he a man-made caricature of evil on which we can blame our own misdeeds. His existence is factual. He must be taken seriously.

The Devil Actively Opposes Christians

The business of the devil is to oppose God. Since God works through Christians, the devil opposes them. Scripture makes this plain. "Be self-controlled and alert. Your enemy the devil prowls around like a roaring lion looking for someone to devour" (1 Pet. 5:8). God provides a description of virtues which together protect against the onslaught of the devil in Ephesians 6:11-17. These virtues are described as "armor." Clearly, there is a battle in which Christians are pitted against the devil. "Resist the devil, and he will flee from you" (James 4:7).

We often think of the devil as dealing mainly with the paranormal—

the frightening stuff of Hollywood movies. This is hardly the case. Concerning the devil and his demons, a prominent theologian wrote, "They hinder man's temporal and eternal welfare—sometimes by exercising a certain control over natural phenomena, but more commonly by subjecting man's soul to temptation."[3] This subtle temptation comprises the bulk of the devil's work:

> How is the devil doing? The divorce rate and disintegration of the Christian family roughly parallels the secular world. Sexual activity among Christian singles is only slightly less. The distinction between a Christian and a pagan is no longer obvious. The tragic fall of many visible Christian leaders indicates that something is dreadfully wrong.[4]

The Devil Actively Opposes the Church

To say that the devil opposes Christians is to say that he opposes the church. After all, Christians *are* the church. There is, however, a special sense in which he opposes the church corporately. He opposes Christians as *individuals*, but also when they band together in cooperation *as a church*. As Neil Anderson, a noted writer in the field of spiritual conflicts, observes, "God has not revealed how the devil has organized and deployed his army for good reason. The devil would just change it. But if you were the devil, wouldn't you spend a good deal of effort directly opposing churches?"[5]

This supposition seems to have broad scriptural support. Charles Mylander points out that Revelation chapters two and three speak of churches and their angels. The context includes more than its share of spiritual struggles. Could these struggles involve demonic attacks? 2 Corinthians 2:10-11 suggests that the devil gets an advantage in a church where there is no forgiveness. To Paul, the devil's involvement in such issues is obvious. He writes, "We are not ignorant of his schemes." When Ephesians 6:11-17 urges Christians to put on the whole armor of God, all of the personal pronouns are plural. Was Paul urging the church as a corporate body to arm itself against the devil?[6] It would seem so.

Few believers would seriously question the devil's active opposition to the church, yet his involvement is often not recognized when it is occurring. His involvement explains so much. People, who because of their mutual faith are bound together beyond any untying, begin to act like enemies. Seldom do they realize that they have become hostages to the puller of strings—puppets in a play directed by their real enemy, the devil.

The Devil Actively Opposes Pastors

Right in the middle of this satanic puppet show is the pastor. The devil opposes the pastor indirectly by promoting conflict, controversy, and hypocrisy in the church. He also opposes the pastor directly: "Strike the shepherd, and the sheep will be scattered" (Zech. 13:7). In many ways, the pastor may be the primary target of the devil when he stirs up strife among others in the church:

> If you are a Christian, you are the target. If you are a pastor, you and your family are the bull's-eye! It is the strategy of Satan to render the church inoperative and to obliterate the truth that we are "dead to sin but alive to God in Christ Jesus" (Rom. 6:11).[7]

God makes the importance of the work of pastors plain in his Word. In addition to the high qualifications listed in the pastoral epistles, James states bluntly, "Not many of you should presume to be teachers, my brothers, because you know that we who teach will be judged more strictly" (James 3:1). Why the stricter judgment? Because those who teach influence the lives of others. Their actions and words have larger consequences than those in more obscure positions. The devil knows this too. This is why he seems to concentrate an inordinate amount of energy attempting to "strike the shepherd."

But I Can't Chart It on Graph Paper!

A seminary professor used to joke about church staff members who became so involved in programs and statistics that they had little time for "real ministry with real people." He used to say, "The best way to make some staff members effective is to take away their desk and graph paper!" There is a broad element of truth in that one liner. In our culture, we seem to have a need to explain and control things. If there is an increasing spiritual challenge in our church, the first answer always seems to be a program. Simply praying about it isn't considered to be enough. In this climate, techniques and twelve-step programs are the order of the day. A recognition that spiritual conflict can never be addressed by a program but only by prayer seems to be beyond us. Eugene Peterson writes:

When I look for help in developing my pastoral craft and nurturing my pastoral vocation, the one century that has the least to commend it is the twentieth. Has any century been so fascinated with gimmickry, so surfeited with fads, so addicted to nostrums, so unaware of God, so out of touch with the underground spiritual streams which water eternal life? In relation to pastoral work the present-day healing and helping disciplines are like the River Platte as described by Mark Twain, a mile wide and an inch deep.[8]

This fascination with gimmickry is part of a cultural bent that tends toward self-reliance and away from any acknowledgment of the supernatural. Many authors have noted this phenomenon. In his book, *The Holy Spirit: Activating God's Power in Your Life*, Billy Graham writes, "Unfortunately, this power has been ignored, misunderstood, and misused. By our ignorance we have short-circuited the power of the Holy Spirit."[9] Chuck Swindoll asks, "Where do you go to find enough stillness to rediscover that God is God?"[10] Charles Ryrie introduces his book on the Holy Spirit with this telling disclaimer:

> If this were a book that offered you some new and startlingly different formula for spiritual power, I am sure the sales of it would be phenomenal. You would probably devour its contents at one sitting. This is not that kind of book, for there is no new and startlingly different formula for spiritual power. There can be nothing new or more added to that which God has already provided.[11]

Our natural approach to the supernatural is to ignore it while we turn our attention to the latest formulas and ministry fads. We arrogantly assume we can deal with the devil through better worship or more self-help groups.

Spiritual conflict cannot be charted on graph paper. It cannot be plotted or predicted. It cannot be programmed away. Nor can we explain the ongoing patterns of dysfunction in churches solely as problems of group dynamics, immaturity, or poor leadership. These may be factors, but there is an unseen hand here: an enemy who is not defeated by our busy efforts. "For our struggle is not against flesh and blood, but against the rulers, against the authorities, against the powers of this dark world and against the spiritual forces of evil in the heavenly realms" (Eph. 6:12).

Spiritual Conflict: The Daily Reality

Spiritual conflict is a *daily* fact of life. Although often not acknowledged except in general terms, the influences of the evil one and his hosts are pervasive, affecting the lives of Christians and churches everywhere.

Individual Spiritual Conflict

Every Christian has his own spiritual pilgrimage and his own struggles to win. The Apostle Paul spoke of the frustration experienced by believers struggling against the downward pull of a world in rebellion to God: "Not only so, but we ourselves, who have the firstfruits of the Spirit, groan inwardly as we wait eagerly for our adoption as sons, the redemption of our bodies. For in this hope we were saved" (Rom. 8:23-24a). Every generation has experienced the same struggle. Martin Luther asserted the inability of human beings to win in this struggle apart from the intervention of God.

> Since, therefore, men, according to the testimony of God Himself, are "flesh," they can savour of nothing but flesh; so far is it from possibility that "Free-will" should do anything but sin. And if, even while the Spirit of God is among them calling and teaching, they only become worse, what will they do when left to themselves without the Spirit of God![12]

This struggle goes on at more than one level. Many temptations and ungodly influences come because we live in a cursed world. Scripture is clear on the subject of who holds temporary sway around here. "As for you, you were dead in your transgressions and sins, in which you used to live when you followed the ways of this world, and of the ruler of the kingdom of the air, the spirit who is now at work in those who are disobedient" (Eph. 2:1-2). Paul speaks of this as an "evil age" (Gal. 1:4). In a world like this, the mere atmosphere produces myriad opportunities for sin of all kinds. The struggle of Christians to live by a value system different from that of the world often seems to lead to a stalemate.

Unfortunately, in addition to the natural temptations of a cursed world, the devil aims his fiery darts at each and every Christian. Paul warned against following the ways of the "ruler of the kingdom of the air, the spirit who is now at work in those who are disobedient" (Eph. 2:2). In the last phrase, he made it clear that some of these unbelievers are not just following the devil's ways. Some are directly controlled by him. The devil assiduously seeks to expand this influence into the realm of Christianity even though he won't ultimately win. This is no illusion or figure of speech. His efforts to influence the church go all of the way back to Ananias and Sapphira (Acts 5:3). He has never given up. Neil Anderson asks three pertinent questions:

1. Have you experienced any temptation this week? Biblically, who is the tempter? It can't be God (see Jas. 1:13). He will test our faith in order to strengthen it, but Satan's temptations are intended to destroy our faith.

2. Have you ever struggled with the voice of the accuser of the brethren (see Rev. 12:10)? Before you answer, let me ask the question in another way. Have you ever struggled with thoughts such as, *I'm stupid*, or *I'm ugly*, or *I can't*, or *God doesn't love me*, or *I'm different from others*, or *I'm going down*? I know you have, because the Bible says that Satan accuses the brethren day and night.

3. Have you ever been deceived? The person who is tempted to answer no may be the most deceived of all.[13]

Corporate Spiritual Conflict

What the Christian experiences individually, the church experiences corporately. The evil one seeks to make the church as ineffective as possible since its work threatens his kingdom. Jesus predicted this spiritual conflict from the outset. "I will build my church, and the gates of Hades will not overcome it" (Matt. 16:18). Charles Mylander suggests several ways in which the devil attacks churches corporately. These include harassment of Christian leaders, financial reverses, conflicts and criticism within the church leadership, promising people moving out of the area with unusual frequency, special attacks on leaders in their own area of temptation, and the age old attack: persecution.[14] Churches can allow the devil a foothold by committing some corporate sin such as factiousness or tolerance of gross sin in the congregation. However, according to Mylander, the devil often attacks for just the opposite reason, wreaking havoc on a church that is doing well and invading his territory.[15]

These corporate attacks are probably at the heart of many churches' ongoing dysfunction. Indeed, they may explain much of the spiritual weakness that seems so prevalent in American Christianity.

Pastoral Spiritual Conflict

The pastor stands at the front lines of defense against the evil one. In addition to waging his own war against the devil, he is there when the devil attacks individual Christians, as well as when he attacks the church as a body. The pastor is in a position where he is targeted by the devil for all three reasons. The devil wants to defeat the believers in his church, he wants to defeat the church as a corporate body, and he wants to defeat the pastor as an individual, thus destroying his ability to lead. Working on the latter can accomplish much for his dark purposes in the other areas as well.

The understanding that pastors are special targets is borne out by research as well as the experience of many. Our survey indicated that personal spiritual defeat was prevalent in one out of four decisions to resign.[16] Spiritual weakness can place a person in a dangerous position. The devil wishes a pastor to feel defeated and has no compunction against kicking him when he is down. Times of discouragement can turn into times of disaster. The devil sees a vulnerable, discouraged pastor and focuses special attacks on him.

Since many pastors have little or no accountability built into their relationship with their church leadership, the threat of spiritual attack is clear. One study indicated that 40% of pastors experienced a "serious relational conflict at least once a month."[17] According to the same survey, 37% of pastors reported "involvement in inappropriate sexual behavior." A similar survey conducted for Leadership found that about one in five pastors admitted to sexual indiscretion.[18] This closely approximates the percentage of pastors from our survey who said they resigned in part because of personal spiritual defeat. The devil's involvement is obvious. How else can one account for this level of indiscretion among people who have given their lives to preach the truth of God's Word?

Many pastors report more overt attacks by the evil one. These include suddenly awakening at precisely 3:00 a.m. terrified (a phenomenon linked to the known activities of witches) as well as unexplained harassment of their children.[19] Depression dogs many ministers and may well represent another of the devil's tools.[20] One pastor and his wife discovered that the only significant tension between them occurred regularly on Saturday night and Sunday morning. When they began to actively resist this satanic attack, the tension evaporated.

In this book we have seen no less than nine areas of struggle for pastors. These include burnout, career isolation, inadequacy of training, unrealistic and ambiguous expectations, lack of accountability, the difficulty of change, financial hardship, personal loneliness, and the ongoing spiritual warfare in which pastors must lead. It is our belief that all of these interact to some extent, but no one area affects all of the others like this last one.

To some extent the devil can use any particularly difficult area as a foothold in a person's life. As a career, the pastorate is replete with such difficult areas. The devil exploits these any way he can. Like all human beings, the pastor struggles with the spirit of this evil age. Because of some of the unique aspects of his job he is tempted to feel sorry for himself or, worse, to chuck his ordination and sell real estate. He is tempted by materialism, laziness, pride, and all of the other things that go with being a fallen human being. In addition, because his job demands a kind of "holy demeanor," he is perhaps uniquely tempted by rebellion and hypocrisy. All of these represent the general work of the evil one. The pastor also faces the specific attacks targeted at him as an individual. These can be devastating. There is no way to quantify exactly the number of pastoral casualties brought about directly by the adversary.

It is important to recognize the true nature of many negative dynamics that create such heartache in churches. One of the more important reasons to do so is to deny the devil the victory over pastors. We can have victory and freedom as pastors and churches, but only when we recognize that there is more to many of our intractable and irritating problems than meets the eye.

We need not be alarmed for Christ has won already, rendering the devil powerless except to deceive. On the other hand we dare not ignore the spiritual forces of darkness in the heavenly realms. It is time for us to recognize who pulls the strings. It is time for us to cut ourselves loose.

You Can Help!

"We are not unaware of his schemes," wrote the Apostle Paul. The devil need not outwit us. We know that he works primarily by lying to us. He is the "father of lies" (John 8:44). We also know that the truth sets us free (John 8:32). We need not be outwitted by the devil. We can find freedom simply by acknowledging and responding to the truth. Neil Anderson offers seven steps to freedom in Christ. These steps are all about dealing with truth. They include renouncing satanic alliances and embracing Christ, renouncing deception and embracing truth, renouncing bitterness and embracing forgiveness, renouncing rebellion and embracing submission, renouncing pride and embracing humility, renouncing bondage and embracing freedom, and, finally, renouncing the sins of ancestors and embracing a new spiritual heritage.[21] These steps do not guarantee permanent victory over the devil. He is a persistent enemy. We must continually acknowledge the truth and live as people who are free in Christ. The devil's only power is in deception. When we embrace truth, his power is broken. You can help your pastor to stand firm against the attacks of the evil one.

1. Pray for your pastor and for your church.

Pray with a recognition that such prayer is spiritual warfare. Many churches have begun to make prayer a higher priority in recent years. Programs like "The Pastor's Prayer Partners" by John Maxwell have become popular. Prayer summits have been attracting increasing numbers of pastors. Men's groups like Promise Keepers emphasize prayer. This is one of the most encouraging developments in recent church history. Become part of it! Pray specifically and continuously for victory over the dark forces that have targeted your church for destruction. Invoke the authority of Christ against them. You can help make a difference for your church and pastor.

2. Commit yourself to spiritual maturity and freedom in Christ.

Maturity and freedom are two different things. Freedom in Christ can be yours instantly by acknowledging the truth and thus resisting the devil. Maturity comes with time, study of the Scriptures, and experience obeying them. Freedom can be gained without maturity, but maturity can never be gained without freedom. Start wherever you are and commit yourself to the truth. You will make a difference. Let the spiritual health of your church begin with you.

3. Avoid any involvement in the devil's classic stratagems.

The devil likes to involve people in gossip, disunity, grumbling, apathy, hypocrisy, and the like. These have effectively hampered churches since Ananias sold his lot and bought the farm. Recognize the spiritual forces at work each time such things begin to occur in a church. Recognize just how much is really at stake. From a pastoral point of view, the work of the ministry slows considerably any time the leadership is forced to "fight fires." Such unproductive effort not only wastes valuable time, but also saps leaders of emotional strength, making them vulnerable to the attacks of the devil.

4. Deal with any corporate sins.

Consider as a church whether or not you need to deal with corporate sins which may be giving the evil one a foothold and creating an ongoing pattern of spiritual defeat in your church. This is a decision for leadership. Neil Anderson and Charles Mylander's book, *Setting Your Church Free*, is an excellent resource offering guidance in diagnosing an ongoing pattern of corporate spiritual bondage, as well as freeing a church from it.

–End Chapter Nine–

[1]Pastoral Survey, see appendix.

[2]Augustus Hopkins Strong, Systematic Theology (Valley Forge, PA: Judson Press, 1907), 454.

[3]Strong, Systematic Theology, 455.

[4]Neil T. Anderson and Charles Mylander, Setting Your Church Free: A Biblical Plan to Help Your Church (Ventura, CA: Regal Books, Gospel Light, 1994), 24.

[5]Neil T. Anderson, lecture presented in "DM 830, Administrative Leadership in the Local Church," 15-19 March 1993, Talbot School of Theology, Biola University, La Mirada, CA, class notes.

[6]Charles Mylander, "Satan's Attacks on Churches," handout, in class notes, from lecture presented in "DM 830, Administrative Leadership in the Local Church," 15-19 March 1993.

[7]Anderson and Mylander, Setting Your Church Free, 24.

[8]Eugene H. Peterson, Five Smooth Stones for Pastoral Work (Grand Rapids: William B. Eerdmans Publishing Co., 1980), 2-3.

[9]Billy Graham, The Holy Spirit: Activating GOD'S Power in Your Life (New York: Warner Books for The Billy Graham Evangelistic Assn., 1978), 14-15.

[10]Chuck Swindoll, "Won't Someone Please Stop Me?" chap. in Come Before Winter ... And Share My Hope (Portland, OR: Multnomah Press, 1985), 317.

[11]Charles Caldwell Ryrie, The Holy Spirit (Chicago: Moody Press, 1965), 9.

[12]Martin Luther, The Bondage of the Will, trans. Henry Cole (Grand Rapids: Baker Book House, 1976), 276.

[13]Anderson and Mylander, Setting Your Church Free, 24-25.

[14]Mylander, "Satan's Attacks on Churches," 2.

[15]Mylander, "Satan's Attacks on Churches," 2.

[16]Pastoral Survey, see appendix.

[17]Richard A. Blackmon, "Survey of Pastors," in "The Hazards of the Ministry," Psy.D. Diss., Graduate School of Psychology, Fuller Theological Seminary, Pasadena, CA, 1984.

[18]David Goetz, "Is the Pastor's Family Safe at Home?" Leadership Journal 13, no. 4 (Fall 1992): 41.

[19]Anderson, "Administrative Leadership," class notes.

[20]C. H. Spurgeon, Lectures to My Students (Grand Rapids: Zondervan Publishing House, 1980), 163.

[21]Anderson and Mylander, Setting Your Church Free, 330-347.

Chapter Ten

Four Facts Of Pastoral Life

PASTORS FACE A SPECIAL SERIES of pressures each week. They result in part from the nine long-term problems which we have discussed and in part from the basic nature of pastoral work. While they do not create so much stress that they scream for attention, they can have a cumulative effect if common-sense safeguards are not in place. These pressures are as follows: pastors are never quite "off duty," they are too often in "crisis mode," they are responsible for more than they control, and they lack an objective measure of success. An examination of these four facts of pastoral life will reveal ways that church members can help.

A Pastor Is Never "Off Duty"

It's not that a pastor never comes home or sits down to relax. It's just that he has at best a limited private life. The modern pastorate is unique among other professions in the degree to which it invades an individual's privacy. This is one of the most often heard complaints about life in the pastorate. H. B. London and Dean Merrill of Focus On The Family's pastoral ministries department write,

> In churches large and small, a delightful topic of conversation is always the pastoral family: what they wear, what they drive, where they go on vacation, how the kids behave, what their house looks like, etc. Though many church folks may not stop to view this from the other side, ministers have a common phrase for it: "life in the fishbowl."

> Pastors start to feel that the congregation not only holds a set of expectations but, in addition, intends to help the pastor and family live up to them. Now, that's pressure! In more than a few churches, of course, the pastoral household never measures up. The inability to be "perfect goldfish" causes them to leave church

prematurely or even to throw up their hands, crying "What's the use?" and leave the ministry altogether.[1]

The modern pastorate is a twenty-four-hour-per-day job that goes beyond the "fishbowl syndrome." There are at least five ways in which the modern pastorate blurs the line between home and work, personal and professional, private life and public ministry. These "cross-over factors" are what make the modern pastorate a total-time job.

Spiritual Discipline Is His Profession

A pastor is considered a professional Christian. The spiritual life with which he wrestles like every other believer is also the subject on which he is deemed an expert. It is the stuff on which his career is built. His personal spiritual well-being and expertise are central to his professional life. After all, he must expound upon heaven and hell, prayer and parenting, angels and abortion—all "as one speaking the very words of God" (1 Pet. 4:11). It is biblical for him to speak boldly of spiritual things. However, because he does so professionally, many people mistakenly count him an expert on life in general, a man with all the answers. When people credit the pastor with this kind of broad expertise, they are blurring the line between the role and the person.

Since the demands of the pastorate are so intense, it is often difficult for the pastor himself to separate his role from his private spiritual journey. There is danger in this. Caleb Colton observes:

> He that studies only men, will get the body of knowledge without the soul; and he that studies only books, the soul without the body. He that to what he sees, adds observation, and to what he reads, reflection, is on the right road to knowledge, provided that *in scrutinizing the hearts of others, he neglects not his own.*[2]

When studying Scripture, it is common for a pastor to find himself preoccupied with the way a given text applies to his congregation, sometimes to one member in particular. Instead of dealing with his own soul, it is tempting for the pastor to say, "Hey, that will preach!" In this way, his personal devotional life is sacrificed on the altar of his profession.

Professionals in a given field are tempted to leave their profession at the office. The result can be that they neglect to provide for themselves and their families in the very area in which they are experts. A pastor who is used to doling out spiritual truth to others can be tempted to neglect it in his own life or to view his personal walk with Christ as a function of his job. Thus spiritual discipline becomes a merely professional matter.

Family Life Is His Profession

Scripture lays out the qualifications for elders carefully. Among them is the stipulation that an elder "manage his own family well and see that his children obey him with proper respect" (1 Tim. 3:4). This passage makes it clear that overseers must be good fathers to their children. This is one way to determine whether or not a man will do well leading in a church. Note that Scripture charges *the pastor himself* with the responsibility of leadership in his home. The leaders of a church have the right and responsibility to assess *the pastor himself* as to whether or not he is doing an adequate job leading his family.

Scripture does not give church members a license to hassle the pastor's family. Somewhere along the line, the spurious notion that a church hires an entire family gained popularity. One can only suppose that it originated with a distorted understanding of the requirement that the pastor be a good father.

> Dr. Thomas Osborne, a psychologist in Wheaton, Massachusetts, says that unlike all other professionals, the clergyman and his family are supposed to reflect the "should do's," while the rest of the world goes about with "do do's." As a layman explained it to a pastor's wife: "We pay you *not* to have problems."[3]

Some church members act as if I Timothy 3:4-5 makes the pastor's entire family properly subject to scrutiny by anyone with the "the gift of criticism." These self-styled pastoral watchdogs love to find fault with his wife's clothes, his children's manners, the family's schedule, or something else. Even among kinder spirits the pastor's family members are counted as examples of all that Christians should be. This means that wherever they are, they feel on display. They are held up to the scrutiny of people who wish to imitate, criticize, or simply notice. They are the "Pastoral Family," the church's hired sample swatches of Christianity.

Social Life Is His Profession

Because a pastor's work is so absorbing, and because his family is counted as an integral part of that work, the family's circle of friends may be largely confined to the church he serves. A pastor carries out many of his most important professional duties in social settings outside office hours.

A price is paid when professional life absorbs social life. Wallace Denton writes:

> One of the problems which I have noted over the years with the minister and his wife is that they often seem to have no peer group to whom they can relate. Another way of saying this is that it appears to me that many ministers and their wives have no group that they regularly interact with where they simply are Bill and Mary. Though most ministers seem to develop close relationships with some parishioners, even in these groups his role as "Reverend Jones" and her role as "the minister's wife" lurks close at hand and tends to obscure the other side of their lives as Bill and Mary.
>
> The loneliness which is regularly reported by ministers' families is directly related to this problem. For loneliness has its genesis not in the absence of people, but in the absence of meaningful and intimate relationships with people.
>
> The lack of a peer group with whom he can let his hair down and give expression to the non-minister side of himself seems to me to be related to fear. As the leader, the minister and his wife are afraid to get too "chummy" with the parishioners whom they lead.
>
> However, since most of the social contacts of the minister and his wife are with parishioners, it presents a real problem as to how they can meet their needs for intimacy. With whom can they share their inner concerns, their doubts, their gripes? Where does the minister meet his need to relate to another human being eye to eye?[4]

No matter how close a friendship between a pastoral couple and anyone in the congregation, it is never quite a normal friendship. The fact that the pastor is the pastor always intrudes. This awkwardness may not be sensed by the other people involved, but it is certainly sensed by the pastoral couple.

Personal Time Is His Profession

In the pastorate, it is difficult to tell how many hours are worked.

This is true for two reasons. First, a pastor works odd hours. He is usually in the office during the day. However, pastoral work in homes and hospitals occurs at varying hours and is required in unpredictable quantities. Further, he often spends evenings in committee meetings. This means that he does not know how many hours he will work each week. Second, pastoral work often mixes personal time with professional responsibilities. A pastor may really enjoy dinner at a church member's home. Nevertheless, he is "on duty," and has the responsibility to listen, care, offer advice, or just be an example. It is also common for the pastor's ministry on Sunday to be considered an additional responsibility beyond the normal workweek. As one church leader put it, "After all, we have to come to church and serve on our day off too." Because there are many hours in a week which are a mixture of professional and personal time, the line between the two is blurred.

Personal Success Is His Profession

How does one define personal success? Men tend to identify it with success on the job. To be a successful doctor, realtor, or contractor equals success in life. That is what mid-life crises are made of. Sooner or later every man learns that there is more to life than the job by which he has defined himself. The Christian world by and large encourages a more balanced view of life. The Bible certainly does: "He has showed you, O man, what is good. And what does the Lord require of you? To act justly and to love mercy and to walk humbly with your God (Mic. 6:8).

For some reason, Christians set aside this thinking when it comes to pastors. The pastorate is unique among professions in the extent to which the pastoral role defines the pastor *as a person*. A dentist may be only fair at his job, but still be considered a highly successful community leader, family man, and all-around nice guy. More to the point, his success as a Christian is never on the line when someone evaluates his skill with a drill. A pastor, on the other hand, is treated like a professional Christian. Therefore, to evaluate his job performance is to evaluate his life. If his preaching is boring or his manner is not what others expect, the evaluation feels like, sounds like, and often is a personal attack. Moreover, a pastor's work consists in large part of building and maintaining relationships. This means that if someone rejects his ministry, it can and often does amount to a rejection of him as a person.

This is an especially acute problem in today's church because people today shop for a church like they would shop for a new car. I have observed that Boomers freely move in and out of several churches, being the most fluid religious generation in American history. Too often today, people wrongly assess a church as if it were a commodity. The critical consumer's eye focuses long and hard on the man in the pulpit. This consumer climate produces tremendous pressure for the pastor. One pastor told of a letter sent to him by a well-meaning churchgoer which suggested that the pastor is "the skin of the church; an example to the congregation of every (!) spiritual gift." Such extreme views are not common (fortunately). What is common in an age of superstars is for people to expect more of their pastor than one man can give. Author Chap Clark illustrates the pain of unrealistic expectations by comparing himself to a fat kid on the track team named Johnny. He finds himself hopelessly outclassed by the other athletes. As he runs his ponderous race, embarrassed friends and family yell, "Johnny, run faster!"

> I am Johnny.

> I've spent most of my life putting on a predesignated uniform, going through my exercises, and running around somebody else's track, on a course I didn't really like—all in the hope that it would somehow make me feel valuable. I have been involved in sports, music, and drama. I have often been popular, successful, and a leader in various groups. But I can still feel myself running, watching people pass me and hearing them laugh and jeer as they race past. Often, out of the stands I hear the voices of those closest to me relationally, telling me how to achieve a better finish in the race. I am tired, I am afraid, and I feel alone.[5]

This analogy often applies to pastors. Church members, with the best of intentions, unwittingly turn up the heat of unrealistic expectations. In today's environment they are exposed to a wider array of ministries, ministry styles, excellent preaching, music and programs than at any time in church history. They would like what they see elsewhere in their church. They communicate these hopes to their pastor in an attempt to be helpful. He is tempted to internalize these suggestions as expectations for which he is personally responsible. "Johnny, run faster!"

When expectations go unfulfilled some church members inevitably leave seeking greener pastors ... we mean greener *pastures*. They seek the best preaching, music, youth group or whatever. Each time someone leaves, the pastor feels the pain of a severed relationship. This is not just a professional setback. It feels like a personal failure.

A pastor is never "off duty." His ministry is his life. Spiritual disciplines, family and social life, personal time, and definitions of personal success all are subjugated to the pastoral role. This integration of personal life with professional would be more tolerable and biblical if the modern pastoral role didn't include ambiguous, unclear and sometimes downright unbiblical expectations. The scriptural role of a pastor is to minister in the sphere of his gifts proclaiming the Word and leading the flock by moral example, to equip others and delegate to them, and to work with other leaders with different gifts. No pastor has all of the gifts needed for balanced leadership in a church. (See chapter 4, "What Do You Expect?" for more on this subject.) Even with biblical expectations of the pastor, he still needs rest from his pastoral responsibilities as part of his obedience to God. He cannot be permanently on duty.

A Pastor Is Too Often in "Crisis Mode"

Today's pastor faces more crises than ever before. Crisis intervention is part of his calling. The pastor knows this, but usually gets more than he bargained for. James D. Berkley writes:

> The call into crisis may be in the middle of the night or in the middle of a meeting. It may come from active church members or from active church avoiders. It may result from something that makes you worry or that makes you weary. Or even wary.

> That doesn't matter. To the parish pastor, the cry of distress will come. Inevitably. Repeatedly. Discomfortingly. People need someone–right now!–and pastors, with hope and a prayer, respond.[6]

The crises which are part of pastoral life are of various shapes and sizes. Some are more intense than others. They tend to have a cumulative effect. There are three basic categories into which these pastoral crises fall.

The Average, Plain-Vanilla, Run-of-the-Mill Crisis

Every profession has its minor crises. They arrive in various vehicles:

deadlines and disgruntled customers, bosses and budgets, co-workers and cash flow. A business must work through all of these things in order to deliver its product and make a profit. These are the average, plain-vanilla, run-of-the-mill crises of any management position. The pastor is no stranger to these. The modern church has all of the trappings of a business. There is a plant to be maintained, a business day to be worked, and customers to keep happy. There is a budget to meet, workers to supervise, and workplace politics to bemoan. There is a market in which, like it or not, a church must compete. This means that the daily workplace crises which affect any business also affect churches and pastors.

There is, however, a difference. Dealing with workplace crises and their resultant stress requires finesse on the part of any manager. In the pastorate, such management is an art form. A church is unlike a business in some very significant ways. It is a volunteer religious organization with constantly shifting relationships and an intangible and frequently ill-defined product. It is tough to manage people if they are not being paid, and tougher if they don't absolutely agree on what it is they are not being paid to accomplish. George Barna describes this aspect of pastoral work.

> A team mentality does not spontaneously arise within a church. A leader must instill the vision for team play among the players and create an environment in which those players work together toward a common end. That objective is to glorify God through acts of personal spiritual growth and community service. Again, using the baseball analogy, the manager may never take the field during the game, but without a strong leader as manager, the team would be undermined by chaos and disunity.[7]

Coaching baseball is child's play compared with coaching a church. On a baseball team, everyone wants to win, and most if not all of the players have some grasp of what it takes to do it. The coach's task is simply to get them to practice the necessary skills and use them together to win. The pastor, on the other hand, cannot assume that his people all have the same definition of victory for the church. One pastor took a survey of his people. He asked one question: "Why does this church exist?" No two answers were alike. In most churches such a question would receive an amazing variety of answers. The pastor is faced with the enormous challenge of turning his people in the same direction before he can even begin the task of coaching them toward corporate victory.

As a manager, he must continually define the product and lead volunteers with various levels of commitment and maturity. Thus, the corporate dynamics inside the average church provide more than their fair share of average, plain-vanilla, run-of-the-mill crises.

The Vicarious Crisis

A pastor experiences more than the minor crises that come with management of a church. The role places upon him the unique responsibility of entering into the various crises of everyone associated with that church and some who wouldn't be caught dead there. It all falls under the heading of "pastoral care." James D. Berkley lists what he considers to be the nine greatest challenges of pastoral care. These include "marital conflict and divorce, sexual misconduct, domestic violence and abuse, homosexuality, major illnesses and injuries, death of a child, death of a spouse, suicide, and alcohol and drug problems."[8] These crises become the pastor's crises because he takes seriously the biblical admonition to "mourn with those who mourn" (Rom. 12:15). Unfortunately, his role in a modern church often goes far beyond these biblical parameters. This is because too many crises are unbiblically funneled his way. He is "the pastor." People ignore the biblical description of that role and mistakenly believe it is the pastor's job to intervene in every crisis.

Pastoral care, as thus defined, is an especially difficult burden for three reasons. First, there is an increasing amount of domestic trauma in our culture. We are reminded of an old mentor who ministered for a decade and a half before ever encountering a divorcing couple. His experience demonstrates that pastoral work in America is *much* tougher today than a generation ago. Churches, and consequently pastors, are on the front line dealing with the social disintegration now apparent in our society.

Second, unlike other helping professions, the pastor must live and maintain ongoing relationships with the people to whom he ministers in times of crisis. A counselor maintains a strict separation between his professional life and his personal life. His clients are his clients and his friends are his friends. This is necessary to his professional objectivity. By contrast, a pastor's "clients" are his friends and co-workers. He lives, works, and socializes with them from week to week. At any given time a pastor is faced with the continual reminders of several current crises among his people—*his people*, not just his clients. The burden can wear him down. Alistair Brown knows what it is to feel that there is nothing more inside to give. He wrote of a time when his church was expanding and spiritual success was apparent everywhere. But the work had taken its toll. One night as a helpful parishioner was recounting the spiritual successes of the church, she beamed, "Alistair, you must be thrilled with all that's happening!" Something inside of him snapped and he replied, "Right now I feel like throwing myself under a bus." With that he burst into tears.[9]

Third, Scripture never intended for pastors to bear the burden of handling every crisis of every member of his congregation. The apostles appointed deacons to deal with a corporate crisis in Jerusalem so that the apostles could devote themselves to "prayer and the ministry of the word" (Acts 6:4). Imagine Peter or James spending hours each week in marriage counseling. Ridiculous! Paul urged Timothy to take seriously his example of purity, the reading of Scripture, teaching, preaching, and the development of his own gifts. He said: "Be diligent in these matters; give yourself wholly to them" (1 Tim. 4:15). Never is Timothy (or any other pastor) instructed by Scripture to bear the sole burden of what we commonly define as "pastoral work." This is one fallacy of our modern spectator approach to church. Every healthy body of believers has in its midst all the necessary gifts to shoulder the burden of caring for itself (1 Cor. 12:7 et al.). The pastor's role is to equip them. If the pastor bears the burden of vicarious crisises alone, he is not only distracted from his real duties, he is headed for danger.

The Personal Crisis

The sad fact is that, sooner or later, too much time spent in "crisis mode" results in a personal crisis. These personal crises range in severity from mild depression to inappropriate behavior. All too often, the church has been treated to the awful spectacle of a burned-out pastor experiencing moral failure.

This is not an isolated problem. One survey found that 75% of pastors had experienced "at least one significant crisis due to stress." The same survey found that 40% had had "a serious relational conflict at least once a month." Astonishingly, 37% reported "involvement in inappropriate sexual behavior."[10] Could it be that living in "crisis mode" wearies a person, breaking down his resistance to temptation and threatening his integrity?

Clearly many pastors lack some key element in managing the crises of ministry. How do other professionals do it? Dr. William Moynihan, a Christian psychologist in Corvallis, Ore., points out that in addition to intensive training designed to help them deal professionally with the crises of their clients, psychologists are accountable to other psychologists. This accountability is part of their code of ethics and an expected part of their professional life.[11] Mike Kirk, a volunteer emergency medical technician, deals with crises regularly on Interstate Five. Asked how he copes with stress, Mike answers,

> Well, we have CIDs (Crisis Intervention Debriefings). We have a sheriff's chaplain who comes in and we talk. It doesn't leave the room so guys just let it all out. Sometimes they cry. Sometimes they apologize for yelling at another EMT while responding to an emergency. Sometimes we just talk about how the call went. Afterward we always feel better.[12]

Training for the average pastor often includes precious little to help him understand and deal with his own response to the constant barrage of pain that is life in the modern pastorate. His attempts to help manage the crises of others often result in his own personal crisis.

A Pastor Is Responsible for More Than He Controls

The modern pastor is credited or blamed for most of what goes on in his church. Yet he controls very little of it directly. Jerry, a member of a small suburban church, told his pastor, Daryl Betts, about a church he had visited where no one greeted or said a word to him. The pastor of that church had called on him the following week. Jerry reported to Daryl that he had given that pastor a piece of his mind. Daryl's unspoken response was, "Why? It isn't his fault. He is probably as frustrated with their unfriendliness as you are!" Should he have taken someone by the hand, led them to the visitor and said, "Now you be polite!"? Or perhaps he should have greeted them himself, thus making up for the failure of the church. He was certainly right at least to talk to that church's shepherd about the problem. Such input is valuable. In time, a pastor can lead a church to be more friendly. Training for greeters and ushers can make people aware of the problem. However, his attitude toward the pastor demonstrated that, to him, the preacher was directly at fault for a failure which, in reality, was not his own. In this way people often blame pastors for problems over which the pastors have no direct control.

149

This identification of the pastor with every aspect of his church sometimes works in his favor, and sometimes not. If he has a praying, friendly church with solid leaders using their gifts as God intended, the church may reach people for Christ and see significant growth. When that occurs, the pastor will be given the credit. However, if a pastor finds a strife-racked body of believers, his church's lack of success will reflect on him. He will likely be evaluated as an average pastor at best. Certainly, he will not receive the same admiration as the man whose circumstances cast him in a better light.

Not only do people inside and outside of the church often have unrealistic expectations of a pastor's leadership, the pastor himself may contribute to these notions.

> Sometimes such unrealistic congregational expectations are the fault of the incoming leader, who has portrayed himself as the answer to all of their problems.
>
> "Looking back on it, I can see where the view that the church had of me was out of proportion to what I could possibly have done," a minister commented during an interview.
>
> "We were a small church with limited funds, and I was a young, energetic seminary grad with lots of ideas and hopes. Unfortunately, they took what I said at face value. They just about expected us to be the new Crystal Cathedral in a few years time. I can't really blame them on that one. I set them up to believe that we would change the world in short order."[13]

A pastor can easily fall into the trap of accepting responsibility for burdens which the Lord never intended he should carry. Stephen Covey speaks of the human tendency to focus on things that cannot be controlled. He says that each person has a "circle of concern." In this circle anything which concerns us can be found. Within this circle is a smaller circle which Covey calls a "circle of influence." In this circle can be found only the things about which we are concerned *and* have some ability to control. He urges people to focus their time and energies upon this smaller circle.[14] Obviously, there is much in a church which is inside a pastor's "circle of concern" but outside his "circle of influence." His all-too-human tendency is to focus energy and emotion on those areas. This is encouraged by an environment which unrealistically attaches him to every facet of church life.

A distorted view of a pastor's accountability before God also contributes to the problem. Peter laid out the proper sphere of responsibility for a pastor. "Be shepherds of God's flock that is under your care, serving as overseers—not because you must, but because you are willing, as God wants you to be" (1 Pet. 5:2). Note first that it is God's flock, not the pastor's. God is at work in each believer's life. Scripture makes it clear that this is His work. "For it is God who works in you to will and to act according to his good purpose" (Phil. 2:13). Note second that the pastor is not called to account for all that goes on in the church but for how well and willingly he performs his task as overseer. That task is adequately defined in the pastoral epistles and does not, as previously noted, include all of the counseling and crisis intervention. Nor does it include responsibility for all of the actions of churchgoers.

A Pastor Lacks an Objective Measure of Success

Jeff, a pastor of a small church in the Northwest, felt glum. Before him on the desk were the numerous notes he had made to himself the week before. Each note reminded him of another task, another area requiring his leadership, another fire to fight. A Bible study needed starting. A conflict needed resolving. Last Sunday's visitors needed contacting. There seemed no end to it. At another time the work would have been invigorating. Today it felt overwhelming. For one thing, no matter how much he did, there was always more to do. There were always more tasks than time. The really disheartening truth was that no matter how hard he pushed himself, nothing seemed to change in his church. People came and went. Issues arose and faded. People spoke of how the church was growing, yet it never seemed to get any bigger.

Jeff is not alone. It has been suggested that as many as half of all pastors feel unable to meet the demands of the job.[15] This is caused in large part by inadequate definitions of pastoral success. If his church is growing it may be easy to define success numerically. But churches don't always grow. Is a pastor therefore a failure? If not, how does he measure his worth as a pastor in the absence of statistical affirmation? If the church *is growing*, do the ever increasing numbers mean that the church and its pastor are doing all that they should do? Is every need being met? Is the church spiritually healthy? All of these questions beg for some concrete definition of success when it comes to the job of church leadership.

There are at least three contributing factors to this lack of an adequate definition for pastoral success. First, much of a pastor's work affects the church only indirectly. Sound administration, carefully planned worship services, and solid teaching may all contribute to conversions, spiritual growth, and an expanding program, but it is sometimes hard to see the direct and immediate connection. Second, many of the factors leading to a church's spiritual success or failure are beyond the pastor's immediate control. Thus, if he measures his own success by that of the church, the results may be misleading indeed. Third, the expectations placed on pastors vary so widely that, if success is measured by meeting expectations, every pastor fails more than he succeeds. Remember that people of differing generations have grown up in different worlds. They therefore have divergent outlooks on life and vastly different expectations of church. Keeping everyone reasonably happy can consume a pastor, making it difficult to slow down enough to ask, "What am I really trying to accomplish here and how will I know when I am succeeding?"

In the absence of a clear definition of pastoral success, many pastors assume that they haven't yet succeeded. They work harder and look for signs of success in a growing church, or in continued congregational affirmation, or in ministry opportunities in more prestigious settings. These are inadequate measures at best.

Pastors need to set some realistic standards for themselves and then measure their success by those standards. Success must be defined as obedience in carrying out the task specifically given the pastor. As Kent and Barbara Hughes define it, success involves faithfulness, serving, loving, believing, praying, pursuing holiness, and being positive.[16] These characteristics of success are not arbitrarily advanced. They are the result of scriptural insight gained during a personal struggle through which the Hughes family persevered in a fledgling church. That crucible experience taught them once and for all that personal success can only be measured by personal actions and attitudes, never by the response of others. More pastors need such liberation. Many find themselves struggling with doubt because they don't measure up to a standard of success which they have not carefully examined. They are hostages to what Hughes called "the goddess of success."[17]

Your pastor may never talk about these issues, but he does face them. They are facts of pastoral life. This is his world. Pastors are never quite "off duty," they are too often in "crisis mode," they are responsible for more than they control, and they often doubt their ability to succeed. They do their best to minister anyway. They want to serve. It only hurts on Monday.

You Can Help

Your pastor will greatly appreciate any help you can offer. Your help will encourage him. It may even help him stay.

1. Affirm your pastor.

Offer him something other than the empty post-service praise that Howard Hendricks calls the "Glorification-of-the-Worm Ceremony." Such compliments, he says, are like perfume, "You inhale the fragrance, but you don't swallow it!"[18] Offer him specific affirmation for the ways in which he uses his personal gifts well in leading the church. Offer him evidence of the ways in which he is effective. This is *thoughtful* affirmation.

2. Create a written job description and define your pastor's success by it.

Be as specific as possible. "Exercise general oversight of all church ministries ..." will not do! You may wish to start with a list of what he is doing now. Pare it down and redirect it until it is a reasonable description of what one pastor can and should do. Ask your pastor to teach you what Scripture says his role should be. Discuss with him his own talents and gifts. You will inevitably limit his role. This is not harmful. It is helpful. In limiting his focus, you will help him to greatly increase his effectiveness. The church will benefit. This process will force you to involve other people in the work of the ministry. That's healthy for both the pastor and the church!

3. Hold him accountable to fulfill his new job description efficiently enough to go home when he is done.

Make sure he takes his days off and also his vacations. Help him guard against unnecessary intrusion into his private life by inconsiderate church members.

4. Help the pastor cope with crisis.

Churches can and should develop a team effort in this area. It should never fall to the pastor alone. Identify people with the appropriate gifts and train them. There is a great deal of resource material to help those who want to learn. At the very least, the leadership should gather around the pastor for a kind of pastoral CID (Crisis Intervention Debriefing). Just knowing that he is not facing it all alone can help tremendously.

5. Develop a small group ministry.

One of the greatest contributions of small groups to the life of the modern church is that they provide a context in which people can give and receive pastoral care *without involving the pastor!* The writer to the Hebrews urged us to "spur one another on toward love and good deeds," and to "encourage one another" (Heb. 10:24-25). If you have only large group gatherings with people in rows facing forward, then this work falls to the man in front. However, if you have small groups where people interact, then they can take up the worthy task to which God calls them. You would be surprised at how much this can relieve the pastor as people get the attention from other believers which they would ordinarily expect from him.

–End Chapter Ten–

[1]H. B. London, Jr. with Dean Merrill, Pastors at Risk: How to Support Your Pastor Through Prayer, Affirmation, and Accountability (Colorado Springs, CO: Focus on the Family, 1992), 3.

[2]Caleb Colton; quoted in Richard J. Foster, Celebration of Discipline: The Path to Spiritual Growth, rev. ed. (San Francisco: Harper & Row, 1988), 62.

[3]Bartlett, The Vanishing Parson 127; quoted in Edward B. Bratcher, The Walk-On-Water Syndrome: Dealing with Professional Hazards in the Ministry, with a foreword by Wayne Oates (Waco, TX: Word Books, Word, Inc., 1984), 85.

[4]Wallace Denton, "Family Conflicts of the Modern Minister," The Baptist Program, March 1974: 7; quoted in Bratcher, The Walk-On-Water Syndrome, 100-101.

[5]Chap Clark, The Performance Illusion (Colorado Springs, CO: NavPress, 1993), 15.

[6]James D. Berkley, Called into Crisis: The Nine Greatest Challenges of Pastoral Care, The Leadership Library series, Vol. 18 (Carol Stream, IL and Dallas: Christianity Today and Word Publishing, 1989), 9.

[7]George Barna, Today's Pastors: A Revealing Look at What Pastors Are Saying About Themselves, Their Peers and the Pressures They Face (Ventura, CA: Regal Books, Gospel Light, 1993), 157.

[8]Berkley, Called into Crisis, 7.

[9]Alistair Brown, "When You Feel Empty," Leadership Journal 11, no. 3 (Summer 1990), 118.

[10]Richard A. Blackmon, "Survey of Pastors," in "The Hazards of the Ministry," Psy.D. Diss., Graduate School of Psychology, Fuller Theological Seminary, Pasadena, CA, 1984.

[11]William Moynihan, interview, 12 February 1995.

[12]Mike Kirk, interview, 11 February 1995, used by permission.

[13]Barna, citing a minister in Today's Pastors, 155.

[14]Stephen R. Covey, The Seven Habits of Highly Effective People: Restoring the Character Ethic (New York: Simon & Schuster, 1989), 83.

[15]Blackmon, "Survey of Pastors."

[16]Kent and Barbara Hughes, Liberating Ministry from the Success Syndrome (Wheaton, IL: Tyndale House Publishers, 1988), 7.

[17]William James; quoted in Vernon C. Grounds, "Faith to Face Failure, or What's So Great about Success?" Christianity Today, 9 December, 1977, 12-13; quoted in Hughes, Liberating Ministry, 10.

[18]Howard Hendricks, "Creativity," continuing education seminar, Auburn, WA, April 1989.

Chapter Eleven

Today Is Friday: Suggestions for Building Up Your Pastor

TODAY IS FRIDAY, my day off. Yesterday was a grueling thirteen-hour day that started with hospital visitation and ended with a wedding rehearsal. Sandwiched in between were administrative responsibilities, study, and just plain "people work." I am tired, but not discouraged. The truth sets us free. When people understand the biblical nature of the church and the role of the pastor in leading it, both the church and the pastor are set free to minister as Christ intended. Such understanding has been the goal of this book; for ourselves, for others called by God to lead the church, and for those who call such men "pastor."

General Observations

There are four common denominators which can be found among the recommendations we've made in this book. Careful attention to these four issues can help your pastor in every area of ministry.

First, you can help by praying. This is old advice but still true. Although sometimes considered cliché, praying invokes the spiritual authority of Jesus Christ. Your pastor needs the divine touch. Praying can not only protect him from many unseen snares, it can contribute decisively to his effectiveness.

Second, you can help by understanding. The professional and personal isolation that your pastor feels because of the special demands of ministry are reduced significantly if he knows that there are people who understand. Even a few simple words from a small number of people can brighten his perspective considerably.

Third, you can help by encouraging. No one needs to be reminded that there are problems in the church, least of all the pastor. On the other hand, we often need to be reminded that there are successes tak-

157

ing place in the church every week. Someone is growing. Someone is encouraged. Someone has been saved. God is at work. Help your pastor to "think on these things" (Phil. 4:8 KJV).

Fourth, you can help by constructive involvement. Use your gift to minister in your church as only you can. Every situation is different, and you alone know what you can and can't do to help your pastor to survive and be effective in ministry. Our challenge to you is to do something. James said, "Anyone, then, who knows the good he ought to do and doesn't do it, sins" (James 4:17).

40 Ways To Help

In each chapter of this book, we have offered simple suggestions as to how you can help your pastor survive and be more effective in ministry. In the interests of simplicity and practicality, this chapter is devoted to a recap of these suggestions followed by some general observations.

Pastoral Burnout

In Chapter 1, "When the Lights Won't Turn On," we saw that those close to the victim of burnout can often see many of these symptoms before he can. If you have some concerns about your pastor, here are some ways you can help.

1. Hold your pastor accountable for stress management disciplines like rest, exercise, and meaningful recreation.

Whether it be Monday or another day, see to it that he takes his days off, and also his vacations. Make sure he actually gets away and does something unrelated to ministry. How will you know if he is really backing off? Simple. Ask his wife.

2. Protect your pastor from spiritual leeches.

Every church has its "clinging vines,"[1] and the pastor is a natural target for them. Surround him with some kind of protection. Perhaps a secretary can make appointments and screen calls. A group of leaders can help bear the load of counseling. Mature church members can take those troublesome and needy souls into their hearts and disciple them, thus lessening their need to depend on the pastor.

3. Get your pastor to go with his strengths.

Everyone has inborn strengths and God-given talents. The problem with the pastorate is that it is often such a generalized role that a pastor can spend an inordinate amount of time working outside the sphere of his gifts. This is always frustrating. Find out what your pastor does naturally well, what he likes to do, and encourage him in that area.

4. Encourage him to fellowship with other pastors.

Isolation contributes to burnout. Gathering with other pastors helps to eliminate the sense of being out there all alone in the pastorate.

Career Isolation

In Chapter 2, "When Are You Going to Get a Real Job?" we discussed the uniqueness of ministry as a career. The pastorate is often misunderstood. This misunderstanding is a source of frustration to pastors who are sometimes tempted to "get a real job." Here are some ways you can help.

5. Recognize the uniqueness of your pastor's job. It is unlike any other.

6. Stop comparing your job to his.

The responsibilities, hours, accountability, corporate dynamics, and even the salary structure, are vastly different. Most comparisons therefore miss the mark.

7. Affirm the value of your pastor's work.

Offer him your support, not just your suggestions. Let him know that you are not waiting for him to slip up, but that you are on his team and are planning to stay there.

8. Pray for your pastor.

He is in a spiritually important and often dangerous place. The enemy has marked him for destruction. Your prayers can shield him from more than you know. Ultimately, these are spiritual struggles. The evil one exploits any opportunity he can, bringing discouragement and a sense of futility. His aim is to thwart the redemptive work of the church. His attack can only be repelled if we do battle on our knees.

Educational Issues

In Chapter 3, "They Taught Us Everything But How to Run a Church," we explored the "education gap." This is the lag that exists between what a pastor learns in seminary and what he actually needs to know to effectively lead a church at the end of the twentieth century. There are several ways to combat this problem. You can help!

9. Encourage or require your pastor to be involved in ongoing education.

This can take the form of substantive seminars or an advanced degree designed to develop proficiency in some area of ministry. The process of mental stimulation can be as important as the material learned.

10. Consider starting an internship program for theological students and/or prospective ministers in your church.

An internship not only represents a biblical model for learning the work of the ministry, but it also represents a practical way to acquaint a student "preacher" with the realities of ministry. This allows a student to benefit more fully from his formal theological education.

11. Be patient with a young pastor as he acquires knowledge that can only be learned through hard experience.

Remember, good judgment comes from experience and experience comes from bad judgment.

Pastoral Expectations

In Chapter 4, "What Do You Expect?" we saw a multifaceted list of pastoral expectations. It is up to the pastor himself to reshape them. You can help him by understanding the problem and encouraging him to deal with it.

12. Ask your pastor to define himself.

If he doesn't, someone else will. Actually, lots of "someone elses" will.

13. Ask him to communicate himself.

If the role of the pastor is to cast vision for the whole church,[2] surely it is up to him to communicate his own role in fulfilling that vision.

14. Ask your pastor to commit himself to doing a few things well.

We have a limited number of talents. If we act the part of the generalist—a jack-of-all-trades—we guarantee that we will be the master of none. We insure mediocrity. If, on the other hand, we focus on our strengths, we will find the path to excellence. Help your pastor to find this path.

15. Ask him to delegate himself.

If he focuses on only a few areas and devotes larger segments of time to them, delegation isn't just desirable, it's essential.

16. Protect him from the pastor abusers.

In every church there is the proverbial squeaky wheel who figures he has a right to as much pastoral "grease" as he can get. Back your pastor up in reshaping the expectations of such people.

Meaningful Accountability

In Chapter 5, "The Invisible Man," we saw that one of the unique facets of a pastor's job is that, while he has many "bosses," he has little supervision. He needs meaningful accountability for maximum performance and for the prevention of many a potential disaster. This is a vital issue.

17. Ask your pastor to work with people rather than alone whenever possible.

This will accomplish several objectives. First, your pastor will become a more effective disciple-maker. Second, others will be encouraged to use their gifts in ministry resulting in a healthier church. Third, your pastor will get to know more people in the church on a deeper level. Fourth, he will not be isolated, but will be spending more of his time in the real world working with real people. This provides a natural kind of accountability.

18. Offer your pastor regular performance reviews.

Many denominations offer questionnaires for this use by the church board. These are excellent tools for judging a pastor's performance by objective standards. Some churches use such questionnaires as a starting point to develop an evaluation instrument tailored to their needs.

19. Enter into a two-way accountability relationship with your pastor based on a mutually acceptable list of criteria.

In this way you can hold each other accountable for specific areas of responsibility without threat. Warning: such lists are only as good as the commitment of the people involved. Honesty and transparency are essential ingredients. Mutual accountability is a useful tool if conscientiously applied.

20. Include your pastor in an accountability group.

This should involve men who take their spiritual walk seriously and are up to the scrutiny. They should be trustworthy men who are capable of keeping a confidence and who do not hold an unrealistic view of pastors as sinners-emeritus.

Transformational Leadership

In Chapter 6, "Stampeding the Sacred Cows," we saw how a change agent frequently gets more than he bargained for. The conflict caused by his efforts to lead the church beyond the status quo has a wearing and telling effect on him. You can offer your pastor help in this worthy effort—help that can mean the difference between spiritual victory and defeat for your pastor and your church.

21. Help your pastor find support.

Ben Patterson lists three sources of support for pastors in times of lonely leadership: "memorizing comfort," "finding Aaron and Hur," and "the support of family."[3] The memorizing of Scripture is one of the areas for which a pastor could be held accountable. At the very least, you could give him some comforting passages and encourage him to memorize them. Aaron and Hur held up Moses' arms during the battle against the Amalekites (Exod. 17:8-13). Every pastor needs such people who will be his strength when his strength is faltering. Holding up his arms could involve simple encouragement, or taking some difficult or tedious tasks off his hands. It should always mean holding him up in prayer. Encouraging your pastor to spend some more time with his family and relatives can also help to restore perspective.

22. Help your pastor find intellectual and spiritual stimulation.

It is essential for pastors to step back from ministry at regular intervals and plug into a battery charger somewhere. One of the biggest mistakes any church can make is to ask a man to lead it into a successful ministry and then fail to equip him with the tools to do so. To put a man in that position is to invite mediocrity, frustration, and discouragement.

23. Get involved in the change.

Change requires more than one voice. To be effective, it must reach "critical mass" and begin its own self-sustaining chain reaction. Many pastors experience only passive support in their efforts to bring change and are therefore frustrated by a committed minority.

Financial Issues

In Chapter 7, "Lord, You Keep Him Humble and We'll Keep Him Poor," we saw that concern over financial matters hamstrings many pastors and provides a strong motivation to seek other employment. This critical issue must be addressed if you want to keep your pastor for a long time. There are several ways that you can help as a church.

24. Realize what is at stake.

Paying a man adequately could spell the difference between having him around long enough to effectively lead or experiencing a pastoral turnover rate that prevents effective leadership from ever taking place. If a poor salary means a high turnover, then a church has been "penny wise but pound foolish."

25. Pay the pastor on the basis of worth not need.

Don't ask him, "How much do you need?" Not only is that question almost impossible to answer because no one can adequately define "need," but it is the wrong basis for determining a pastor's salary. I Timothy does not say "double what he needs." On the contrary, it commands double honor for a job well done.

26. Find ways to eliminate "apples and oranges" comparisons in the area of salary.

For specific suggestions on how to accomplish this, see chapter 7.

27. Allow God to bless you for your generosity.

Remember there is no command in Scripture to err on the side of caution when it comes to generosity. In this particular area, a little generosity could return to you ten-fold through the efforts of a more effective and long-lasting pastor.

Personal Loneliness

In Chapter 8, "Friend or Flock?", we saw that a pastor is socially isolated in the midst of a large circle of churchgoers to whom he offers friendship but from whom he cannot accept it back in full measure because of the constraints of his vocalist. Pastors need care from other humans. In this area, you can help.

28. Offer relational support.

Let him know that you are not surprised or disappointed by his humanity. One way to do this is to provide him with opportunities for recreation in an atmosphere not dominated by ministry concerns.

29. Honor your pastor's need for privacy.

This means keeping church business inside office hours as much as possible, guarding his days off, and making sure he gets away from time to time.

30. Don't begrudge him his friendships.

If the pastor has an outside social life and friendships with others that are closer than with you, recognize that this is entirely reasonable and healthy.

31. Encourage his involvement in extracurricular activities such as sports or hobby clubs.

Express your encouragement in this area based on his needs, not on the need to meet people for the sake of evangelism or ministry. Sometimes he needs to be just another person.

Spiritual Conflict

In Chapter 9, "The Puller of Strings," we saw that behind many of the repeated patterns of spiritual defeat in a given church lies our enemy, the devil, evilly manipulating the situation with the skill of a puppeteer. One major target, perhaps the major target, is the man who leads. You can make a difference in this battle.

32. Pray for your pastor and for your church.

Pray with a recognition that such prayer is spiritual warfare. Pray specifically and continuously for victory over the dark forces which have targeted your church and pastor for destruction. Invoke the authority of Christ against them.

33. Commit yourself to spiritual maturity and freedom in Christ.

Let the spiritual health of your church begin with you.

34. Avoid any involvement in the devil's classic stratagems: gossip, disunity, grumbling, apathy, hypocrisy, and the like.

These have been effectively hampering churches since Ananias got into the real estate business.

35. Consider as a church whether or not you need to deal with corporate sins.

Unresolved sins can cause problems for churches as much as for individuals. Such sins can give the evil one a foothold and create an ongoing pattern of spiritual defeat in your church.

Weekly Pressures

In Chapter 10, "Four Facts of Pastoral Life," we saw that, as a result of the issues we have been exploring, most pastors struggle to some extent with four weekly pressures. First, the pastor is never quite "off duty." He may show up at his house. He may even spend an adequate amount of time there (though many don't), but he is always "on call" and, in the minds of many, always on the job. He therefore never lays down the burden entirely. He's never quite "home." Second, he is too often in "crisis mode." This is in large part a result of our modern crisis-ridden churches. Third, in an environment of multicultural ministry expectations, he is responsible for more than he controls; and, fourth, like many other pastors, he never knows when he is finished. You can help.

36. Affirm your pastor.

Offer him specific input on the ways in which he uses his personal gifts well in leading the church. Offer him evidence of the ways in which he is effective. In other words, offer him *thoughtful* affirmation.

37. Create a written job description and use it to define your pastor's success.

Be as specific as possible. This process will likely force you to involve a few other people in the day-to-day work of the ministry. This is healthy for both the pastor and the church.

38. Hold your pastor accountable, not only for fulfilling the job description, but also for doing it efficiently enough to go home when he is done.

Find ways of guarding him against unnecessary intrusion into his private life by inconsiderate church members. Make sure he takes his days off and also his vacations.

39. Help your pastor cope with crisis.

Churches can and should develop a team effort in this area so that crisis intervention is not the task of the pastor alone. Identify people with the appropriate gifts and train them. There is a great deal of resource material to help those who want to learn. At the very least, the board should gather around the pastor for a kind of pastoral CID (Crisis Intervention Debriefing). Just knowing that he is not facing it all alone can help tremendously.

40. Develop a small group ministry.

One of the greatest contributions of small groups to the life of the modern church is that they provide a context in which people can give and receive pastoral care *without involving the pastor!* The writer to the Hebrews urged us to "spur one another on toward love and good deeds," and to "encourage one another" (Heb. 10:24-25). These are natural tasks for small groups and often relieve the pastor of burdens he otherwise would bear alone.

–End Chapter Eleven–

[1]H.B. London, Jr. & Neil B. Wiseman, Pastors at Risk: Help for Pastors, Hope for the Church (Wheaton, IL: Victor Books, Scripture Press Publications, 1993), 170.

[2]Rick Warren, Defined Purposes: How to Lay a Foundation for Growth, Audio tape of message by Rick Warren, presented at the 1990 Saddleback Church Growth Conference (Mission Viejo, CA: The Encouraging Word).

[3]Ben Patterson, "The Pastor as Lightning Rod," chap. In Who's in Charge? Standing Up to Leadership Pressures, by Leith Anderson, Jack Hayford, and Ben Patterson, Mastering Ministry's Pressure Points series (Sisters, OR: Multnomah Press Books, 1993), 46.

Afterword for Pastors

PASTOR, IF YOU ARE SUFFERING in your current ministry, there is hope. The person with the greatest power to affect your situation is you. While this book has focused on the many ways that churches could improve their pastors' lot, thereby allowing them to minister more effectively over a longer period of time, only you know what changes would make a difference in your particular case. Perhaps the answer to your problems lies not in an updated resume, but in an updated relationship to your church. Why not be the one to break the pattern? The church will be healthier as a result, and so will you.

Danger: Martyr Crossing

A cartoon in *Leadership* depicts a pastor walking down the street encumbered with a series of heavy balls and chains. He wears a look of exaggerated despair. Two members of his congregation look on but seem unconcerned. One of them remarks, "Looks like Pastor White's going through another trial."[1] The germ of truth that makes this cartoon funny is the tendency of some pastors to adopt the role of the martyr.

Consider, for example, the matter of pastoral salaries. Many pastors complain of the financial hardships they endure in the ministry. Yet if you were to ask, "Have you talked to your board about this?" many would reply, "Oh no! I would never complain about money to my board." This is martyr thinking. A pastor giving this answer would have some seemingly good reasons for his silence, such as: "The Lord provides." While this is true, there may be other dynamics at work. The pastor may be afraid of looking greedy. He may be afraid of creating conflict. (Imagine that.) He may simply be too proud to "beg." Whatever the reason, he deems being underpaid a more attractive option than coming clean with a forthright boardroom discussion of the issue from a biblical perspective. He would rather be a martyr.

Martyrdom in this area has some subtle advantages. A low salary allows a pastor to feel a certain sense of moral security. At least he knows he isn't in it for the money. It may even provide a sense of moral superiority. "I do a lot for a little. I do it for the Lord. I am one of the committed and am willing to suffer for the cause of Christ!" Interestingly enough, this nobility doesn't stop him from sensing the Lord's leading to a church offering a more attractive salary package.

A low salary can also go some distance toward assuaging one's guilt over any laziness or inefficiency in his work habits. If his church doesn't pay a decent wage, he can more easily assure himself that a merely adequate effort (as opposed to his best effort) is acceptable. Once again, this tacit agreement to mutual mediocrity doesn't stop a man from seeking greener grass.

Such thinking can occur when a pastor faces any problem in his church. It is easier to let it slide and feel that odd combination of self-pity and self-congratulation than it is to deal honestly and firmly with the issue. A pastor may jump through hoops to meet as many diverse congregational expectations as possible. He will feel harried, put-upon, and resentful, but also indispensable and a bit smug. He is a martyr.

So what is wrong with being a martyr? Plenty. It is one thing to suffer at the hands of Christ's enemies—to be punished for doing good. It is quite another to suffer relatively minor and largely preventable frictions and inconveniences in a Christian community. This latter state of affairs flies in the face of scriptural principles dealing with unity and harmony in the body of Christ, not to mention passages that deal directly with the pastor-church relationship. By not coming clean about the nagging problems he faces, a pastor may give himself a sense of selflessness, but he robs his church of the blessing and growth that would come with addressing the real issues. He also allows a detrimental working environment to continue wearing him down. The end result may well be a premature move to another church or, worse, a burned out and embittered ex-pastor—the ultimate martyr.

Changing Churches vs. Changing Your Church

While there are valid reasons to change churches, in most cases changing the church you are in right now is a better option. Count carefully the cost of a ministry move. Changing churches means giving up the relationships you have worked hard to build with key people in your current ministry. You will have to start from scratch. It means adjusting to a whole new set of expectations which, even with the best candidating process, can only be guessed at. Making so major a change also creates an instability in the pastoral family that simply cannot be ignored. Moreover, moving often entails significant financial sacrifice. Real estate commissions, closing costs, and other expenses associated with establishing a new home can be enormous.

Perhaps the greatest cost of all is the price of stunted professional growth. By starting over, a pastor robs himself of the experience that comes with a longer tenure. He simply repeats his current experience in another place. Remember Bratcher's assessment:

> It has been said, that it is far more honest for a pastor who has been in the ministry for fifteen years to say that he has had three years' experience five times over rather than to say that he has had fifteen years' experience.

> Short pastorates have not only kept ministers from developing skills which come from length of time in one location, but have also made it possible for ministers to continue to make the same mistakes over and over again. Bad habits developed in the first pastorate are often repeated in the second, third, and fourth.[2]

Clearly, changing churches can be a costly solution to a problem pastorate. There is another way. You can change the church in which you currently minister. Stephen Covey's "circle of influence"[3] applies here. By focusing on those areas in which you have influence, you can make a difference in your relationship to your church. Is the problem you face one of clashing expectations? Before you resign over the issue, sit down and have a friendly but frank discussion of the subject with your leaders. Help them to see the impact of cumulative expectations. Work with them to address the problems. Is the church resistant to your leadership? Bear in mind that it will probably take you less time and effort to overcome resistance here than to establish credibility and effective leadership in another church. Moreover, you will grow through the experience.

You know more about virtually every area addressed in this book than even the wisest member of your congregation. Therefore, you have the greatest ability to focus attention where change is needed. You have more influence than you may think. Use it. Don't just change churches, change your church! God's Kingdom will benefit and so will you.

–End Chapter Twelve–

[1]Rob Portlock, cartoon in <u>Leadership Journal</u> 6, no. 2 (Summer, 1985): 47.

[2]Edward B. Bratcher, <u>The Walk-on-Water Syndrome: Dealing with Professional Hazards in the Ministry</u>, (Waco, TX: Word Books, Word, Inc., 1984), 164.

[3]Stephen R. Covey, <u>The Seven Habits of Highly Effective People</u> (New York: Simon & Schuster, 1989), 82f.

Appendix

Contributing Causes Of Pastoral Resignations

Contributing Causes	According to Pastors	According to Churches
Resistance to pastoral leadership	63%	67%
Unwritten expectations of the pastor	47%	43%
Resistance to change	43%	50%
Corporate spiritual defeat	43%	33%
Burnout	40%	43%
Conflict within the decision-making body	40%	37%
Disagreement over church polity	33%	17%
Salary issues	30%	13%
Personal loneliness	30%	27%
Doubt about call to ministry	27%	30%
Personal spiritual defeat	27%	27%
Lack of pastoral accountability	23%	23%
Disagreement over theology	17%	20%
Inadequate education	17%	13%
Unwritten expectations of the pastoral family	10%	27%
Inability to meet a written job description	10%	0%

The McIntosh Church Growth Network

In 1989 Dr. Gary L. McIntosh founded the **Church Growth Network**, a consulting firm which assists churches to reach their greatest effectiveness in finding, keeping and building new people.

The Church Growth Network conducts individual consultation with churches with specialization in the areas of generational change, analysis of church health, and long range planning.

The popular *Church Growth Network Newsletter* is read by approximately 10,000 pastors and church leaders each month. In a short, highly readable format, the *CGN newsletter* focuses on issues and answers for leaders of todays churches.

For complete information, please contact Dr. Gary L. McIntosh at

> The Church Growth Network
> PO Box 892589
> Temecula, Ca 92589-2589
> Phone or fax 909-506-3086

Other Exciting Products from ChurchSmart Resources

Natural Church Development

By Christian Schwarz

In an attempt to put denominational and cultural distinctives aside, the author has researched 1000 churches in 32 countries to determine the quality characteristics that growing, healthy churches share. Schwarz's research indicates that quality churches score high in eight quality characteristics, but will only grow to the level that their minimum factor (or lowest of these eight characteristics) will allow them. This book is a must read!

ChurchSmart price $19.95

Raising Leaders for the Harvest

By Robert Logan & Neil Cole

Raising Leaders for the Harvest introduces the concept of Leadership Farm Systems, an organic process of leadership development which results in natural and spontaneous multiplication of disciples, groups, ministries and churches. This resource kit includes six audio cassettes and an action planning guide with worksheets. Discover how to raise leaders in your church for the harvest in your community!

ChurchSmart price $60.00

Focused Living Resource Kit

By Terry Walling

Focused Living is a personal development process designed to help believers bring strategic focus to their life and ministry. Focus is obtained by examining their past (Perspective – Personal Time-Line), clarifying their future (Focus – Personal Mission Statement) and identifying resources that will facilitate future growth and effectiveness (Mentoring – Personal Mentors). This resource includes six audio cassettes, three self-discovery workbooks and a leader's guide.

ChurchSmart price $60.00